Mine honor is my life: both grow in one;
Take honor from me, and my life is done.

William Shakespeare

On my honor, I will do my best
to do my duty to God and my country.

Boy Scouts of America

Biography

As a young man Colonel Elmo 'Mo' Baker, USAF (Ret.) had an intense love of flying. A ride in a carney Piper Cub, twice around town was all it took to start 16 year old Mo Baker off on a life of adventure with flying. He knew at that early moment he was meant to fly jets. Diligently, he took the tedious steps necessary to land him eventually in the cockpit of an F-105 Thunderchief (Thud.)

He arrived at Takhli, RTAFB, Thailand, in March of 1967. Already a seasoned aviator with over 3,000 hours flying jets he soon found himself over North Vietnam bombing strategic targets in the infamous Route Pack 6. On August 23, then Major Mo Baker after flying sixty-one missions over North Vietnam was shot out of the sky by enemy anti-aircraft fire. Thus began a five and a half year ordeal of survival in the prisons of North Vietnam, including the infamous Hanoi Hilton.

Serve With Pride & Return With Honor, chronicles his journey to the skies over Hanoi and the brutal existence experienced as an American Prisoner of War. Torture, neglect, mistreatment, and humiliation were staples of his years held as a prisoner of the North Vietnamese. The character and perseverance of the American military man is presented in the stories and impressions emblazoned on his soul. Many have told their story of similar experiences. Many are much more detailed. However, few share the story with the compassion and clarity of Mo Baker.

Eventually, Mo Baker was released with the other 601 returnees. In the forty year interval between that release and now, these memories have existed as vignettes, surfacing as impromptu talks, sporadic articles to interested public and civic organizations, and workshops to military personnel. **Serve With Pride & Return With Honor** now assembles these memories in a single, concise, and comprehensive account.

As a result of his service to his country, Colonel Elmo 'Mo' Baker is a highly decorated hero. He has been awarded the Silver Star with three Oak Leaf Clusters, Bronze Star with one Oak Leaf Cluster, Distinguished Flying Cross with three Oak Leaf Clusters, Air Medal with ten Oak Leaf Clusters, Purple Heart with one Oak Leaf Cluster, and Combat Campaign Ribbon with fourteen Oak Leaf Clusters.

After Vietnam, Mo returned to a normal life, eventually retiring from the Air Force in 1978. He raised a family of four children and now lives with his wife Honey in the small Texas City of Burleson. By all accounts he lives a blessed life, of which there was little hope in the dungeons of the Hanoi Hilton. His gratitude and respect for those airmen with which he served knows no bounds. The memory of flying wing tip to wing tip with them will forever be recorded in this volume, for together they **served with pride and returned with honor**.

Serve With Pride

&

Return With Honor

A Hanoi Hilton Odyssey

The POW Experiences of

Colonel Elmo "Mo" Baker USAF (Ret.)

mobaker2m@yahoo.com

Dedication

To the brave and loyal military wives who put their lives in limbo and waited years and years for their POW to return.

Upon my release from prison I met one of those who lost her husband in Vietnam but waited seven and one half years to see if he might be among the returnees. I married, Marjorie "Honey" Connolly, the widow of Lt. Col. Vince Connolly, who was killed in action (KIA), 4 Nov. 1965. We have happily shared our lives for forty years.

Acknowledgements

I gratefully acknowledge the assistance and Trojan work of Dan Boutwell; friend, neighbor, fellow Rotarian, and author of his own books. Dan used his skills in organizing and editing to assemble the scattered notes I have written over the past forty years into what you see published today. He was tireless, meticulous, and continually inspirational. I could not have done it without him.

I also feel compelled to acknowledge the deep affection and gratitude I have for Colonel Larry E. Carrigan, USAF (Ret) who shared cells with me which, at times were no larger than a normal bathroom. Larry's courageous, un-intimidated, and indomitable spirit kept me from taking prison life too seriously during our years together. Larry has a great sense of humor. Together we laughed our way through some dark days in the Hanoi dungeons.

My thanks go to Captain John M. McGrath, USN (Ret), author of *Prisoner of War, Six Years in Hanoi,* and his publishers, Naval Institute Press, for the use of Mike's sketches of three scenes in the prison in Hanoi. Mike is a past president of our fraternal organization, Nam-POW Inc. He is the historian of Nam-POW and has the complete data on our tenure in his "Macs Facts". He is the infallible authority on who was there and where they lived during their stay. He doesn't like mistakes.

Many thanks go to my comrade-in-arms, Lieutenant Colonel John Piowaty USAF (Ret), for proof reading my draft and keeping me straight on the air battles we fought. John is a meticulous record keeper and can tell you the time over target (TOT) of every one of the 100 missions he completed in Vietnam.

He and I fought in other peoples' wars as well. We flew in the Iran Contra Affair for Ollie North and in Columbia SA helping locate the insurgents ELN and FARC. John is an author too. He loves a good yarn and wrote a collection of his own titled, *Stories for the Telling,* published by Mill City Press.

Input from four dear friends who are not flyers was greatly appreciated. In a discourse centered on the technology of air war and human conflict the details of family and everyday life are sometimes neglected. Brenda Gammon, Terri Herrera, Sally Tomlison, and Maxi Millican were gracious and patient in their proof reading of this book, and I am grateful to them for their attention.

And, I appreciate the comments and review of Hubert Ruff and another author, David McClain. Both of these men are Vietnam veterans who witnessed the conflict at eye level and are friends of my associate, Dan Boutwell. In David's case it is certainly an honor to get a "well done" from a professional.

Table of Contents

Table of Contents Continued

Table of Contents Continued

Foreword

The accounts provided within these pages are stories of an ordinary individual who has experienced extraordinary conditions. I have often had people tell me they could never have survived the ordeal of being a captive in the dungeons of Hanoi. That simply is not true. They are made of the same stuff that I am. I had a Tom Sawyer boyhood in a small Midwestern American town. In Kennett, Missouri, the entire village knew one another, including their parents, brothers and sisters, and even the family dog. There was no terror or hatred in the formative years of my childhood which equated to that I encountered in North Vietnam. Life in Kennett was characterized by a cozy feeling of belonging and security. The *Hanoi Hilton* was a hell where the prisoner was on the brink of violent, painful death at the whim of a Godless captor. And yet, I was able to meet those fears and threats head-on with the confidence instilled in me by my American heritage, the same heritage which we all possess.

The following pages contain the happenings and events as I remember them. It has been over forty years since I experienced these events. So many of them are burned solidly into my memory such that they are as fresh to me as if they happened today. However, many of the stories have been told time and again until they have become a part of my very being. In addition, I share these accounts with a band of brothers and have even fogged the memory such that I have at times forgotten just who the real participant was, though often it may have been me. If during the telling of these accounts it appears I have taken credit for something or incorrectly assigned credit to others, well please forgive me. The accounts herein have so filled my life with rich memories that they have all become an indelible part of me.

It is my deep belief that our warriors go to battle armed with power that is awesome to our enemies. First is the very important power we have in our religious heritage--the simple faith that we all believe there is a God, He knows us, and we are important to Him. I will relate experiences showing how powerful that heritage really is.

Secondly, we enter the conflict with the power of our national character, which is self-assured and independent, and causes men to stand taller than they ever thought possible. We hold individuals to be important in our country. We cannot easily be stripped of our self-esteem. I firmly believe none of the enemy's attempts to denigrate us were effective. Though they labeled us as being *black criminals*, forced us to bow to their guards and officers, and refused to use our names or ranks, we refused to be demoralized. We had full confidence our nation had not forgotten us nor would they allow us to remain captive forever.

Lastly, the training given to warriors of the Armed Forces of the United States was then and is now without equal. Through every moment of my capture I felt the enemy was behaving in a predicted manner, the manner we had learned in our survival training before entering the combat zone. I did not look forward to the cruelty of the enemy's interrogation; but neither was I surprised by it. I had learned many ways to minimize it.

In the end, the North Vietnamese found their approach to dominating the American prisoners through torture and deprivation as being counter-productive. They found that Americans were extremely patriotic and valued their national honor far above their own personal safety and comfort. They discovered application of excruciating pain may force an American soldier to yield to the immediate demands of the torturer; but the next attempt to gain cooperation became more and more difficult.

Further, the information gained by the enemy was highly unreliable and was seldom of any value. Following the death of Ho Chi Minh in September of 1969, the tough leaders of the North Vietnamese abandoned their harsh and inhumane treatment of the American prisoner.

Our motto as American prisoners was **Return With Honor**. The 601 POWs who returned from the dungeons of Hanoi, in the spring of 1973, did so with heads held high and as proud to be an American as ever before. I am privileged to have served with those men.

Chapter 1
FIRST THINGS

I had dodged the "golden B-B" too many times. The odds caught up with me. My F-105D-Thunderchief (Thud) took two hits in the belly while going down the chute at six hundred knots. The Bac Giang Bridge northeast of Hanoi was my target. But I was the target for 138 adrenaline-fed North Vietnamese anti-aircraft gunners. The "idiot panel" of emergency warning lights, lit up like a Christmas tree as my aircraft began to come apart. It screamed out nonsense readings such as GEAR DOWN and OXY LOW, meaning I was hit in the electronics bay just behind the cockpit. As bad as that sounds, it is not the worse that could happen. The worst that could happen was for the forward fuel cell above and aft of that bay to take a hit, which it did. It spewed jet fuel around the engine shroud and tailpipe like a severed artery. I torched!!! All of Vietnam could see the fire plume. (The best I can describe it is that it looks like a shuttle craft launch to see a Thud light up).

I pickled (dropped) the two three-thousand-pounders directly on the center of the bridge and attempted to pull out of the screaming dive. The stick felt limp and impotent. The hydraulic pressure went to zero before I could get the nose up. To break the dive I deployed the RAT, a small Ram Air Turbine that provided emergency hydraulic pressure. When that emergency pressure was depleted, I electrically locked in the elevator slab and leaned back to take stock of the situation. My aircraft was now a high-powered, unguided missile streaking through the North Vietnamese sky at greater than 550 knots in a three-degree nose-low attitude. I had no control over the fate of the aircraft. That was not a good place to be.

I called "Shark Three has been hit," which was not news to the

1

thirteen Thuds behind me who had just seen their leader torch.

"I've got to punch out; see you guys after the war," I said a moment before I ejected.

I separated from the ejection seat, my main chute deployed, and I drifted slowly towards the earth below. Like Alice stepping through the Looking Glass I stepped into another world. And, like Dorothy in Oz I too would soon confirm that "We were not in Kansas anymore." But, in my case it was Missouri. This was indeed a long way from home.

Home

I was raised in a farming community located in the Mississippi River delta. Kennett, Missouri, had a population of around twelve thousand people. Economic geographers call such towns *Rural Agrarian Service Centers.* The boot-heel of Missouri was checkered with these towns every fifteen miles or so. Cotton was the principal crop in my formative years. From an early age I chopped the weeds from the cotton rows in the spring and picked cotton in the fall. In between times I worked in the department stores each Saturday selling overalls and plaid shirts to the farming families.

My father was the Metropolitan Life Insurance agent for the surrounding area, where he earned a good living for his family. There were four boys and a girl in our family. I was the third child. Those were the happy days from 1936 to 1950. In High School I excelled in academics and joined every extracurricular activity I could. It was a way to keep life interesting in the flat lands. I was not beefy enough to play football so I joined the marching band. It was a marvelous move. The band had its own camaraderie where I made deep and lasting friendships.

My interest in flying began as a six year old lad. For Christmas that year my parents bought me a kit that had an airliner dash board embossed full of impressive instruments as well as a yoke with a steering wheel with buttons to push for the imaginary radio. I had great fun lining up the family dining room straight-back chairs and playing pilot. I coerced neighborhood playmates to sit in the line of chairs and accept orange juice from one of my female chums acting as the flight attendant. As the pilot, I sat in the lead chair making mandatory position reports and occasional announcements to the passengers about the foul weather ahead.

At age sixteen I had my first real experience flying. While attending the 4th of July celebration of 1948 in Piggott, Arkansas, as a cornet player with the Kennett Band, I had an opportunity to ride the front seat of a Piper Cub twice around the town for the astronomical price of five dollars. I had saved this sum from my part-time jobs and was not at all reluctant to pay the price. I was thrilled, and I was hooked. From that moment on, somehow or another, I planned to do a lot of flying in my future. My father was not surprised when I told him about the adventure. He could see the sparkle in my eyes.

He said, "Son, one day you will fly a plane as naturally as I drive the car."

World War II (WWII) commandeered the efforts of everybody in the USA to help out in some way from 1941 to 1945. As a teenager, I helped with the family victory garden. We raise chickens in our back yard since food was rationed. We bought ten-cent saving stamps and pasted them in books to aid the war effort. RKO produced news reels about the weekly war progress. There were gun-camera clips of P-51 Mustangs strafing enemy steam engines and dramatically pulling up through the steam from the ruptured boilers. Those men were my heroes. I had to be among them someday. Graduating from High School in 1950, I accepted a Curators Scholarship for two years of free tuition to the University of Missouri. I had not forgotten my quest to fly. As a matter of fact, my passion burned even brighter.

Peace from WWII did not last long. By the time I entered college US forces were engaged in a *police action* to drive back North

Korean Communists from their invasion of the southern part of that country. The news reels were full of gun-camera clips of the F-86 Sabers shooting fifty caliber busts into the fleeing MiG-15s. I had to prepare. Two years of college was a mandatory requirement before one could apply for the United States Air Force (USAF) Aviation Cadets.

My window of opportunity came the summer of 1952. I was just one year away from launching my aviation career when in 1953 the hostilities in Korea ceased and peace accords were signed. I was shocked. Was my master plan to be a jet ace destroyed? It was selfish of me to not rejoice at the peaceful conclusion of the conflict in Korea. But what chance did I then have of being among the flying aces of the USAF?

As I plowed through the second year of college, I noticed significant changes occurring in the military. The reservists who were called to active duty to fight in Korea returned home and resumed their civilian life. Moreover, there was a reduction in force to trim the military population to peace time levels. People were being required to leave the active duty forces or accept a lower rank to continue on duty until their retirement eligibility was met. I thought surely the Aviation Cadet Program, which produced 2000 graduates per year, would cease since pilots were no longer required in great numbers. Happily, I was wrong.

The active duty pilot population of the Air Force depleted more rapidly than anticipated. Pilots on active duty at that time believed promotions would be slow in peace-time. And, the austere budgets of peace-time operations reduced the appeal for continuing their careers. Civilian aviation, however, was booming and the airlines offered generous salaries to experienced pilots. The active duty pilots of the armed forces exited in large numbers. Consequently, the Aviation Cadet Program remained open and I still had the chance to obtain a million dollars' worth of flight training, a commission to second lieutenant, and pilot wings, which would allow me to reach my dream of flying jet fighters.

USAF Aviation Cadet

I returned to Kennett in May 1952 with two years of college credits and an eager desire to launch my flying career by becoming an aviation cadet in the United States Air Force. The Air Force recruiter agreed I had the academic requirements but indicated they would not likely have an opening for six months. The Selective Service was also eager to draft me to meet their quotas for that summer as well. On the advice of the recruiter, I enlisted in the Air Force as an enlisted man to avoid being drafted into the Army. I entered the basic training program at Lackland AFB, San Antonio, Texas, in June of 1952. Immediately, I sought a slot for aviation cadets. By the time I finished boot camp in Lackland AFB, I was accepted and slotted to begin preflight training in January of 1953. At last I was on my way to becoming a pilot.

Preflight training at Lackland AFB was very similar to the sixteen weeks of basic training I had just completed. We were restricted to the base, taught to march (remember, I had four years in the marching band in high school and was fresh out of basic training where we marched daily,) and schooled in the ethics and code of conduct of military men.

Following preflight training, we were sent to contract schools for basic pilot training. I was sent to Bainbridge, Georgia. There a contractor, Southern Airways Aviation, taught us the fundamentals of flying as well as the essentials of weather forecasting and instrument flying. Their curriculum started with a twenty flight-hour program of flying the PA-28, Super Piper Cub. This phase of training was to identify students who were totally unsuited for flying due to coordination problems or had chronic motion sickness. I hated to see some of my new friends failing to reach their dreams.

"Haden," I said to one of my fellow cadets,"I don't want to see you leave. When you fly, try not to think about getting sick."

"I don't think about it!" Haden insisted. "Until I start puking. Then I am reminded of it!"

Some people are simply not cut-out for aviation. Several of our small group were *washed out* and reassigned without prejudice to a base of their choice. Personally, I was far too excited at being there and actually flying to think about motion sickness. I soloed promptly and learned *power-on* stall recovery and *power-off* recovery. I learned to put the aircraft into a spin and recover at will. The twenty hours of flight time passed quickly and we moved on to a larger, more demanding trainer, the T-6 Texan.

The Texan was a tail dragger with retractable gear, a 625 horse-power engine, and a nasty habit of ground looping when landing without precision and caution. My instructor was a former WWII P-39 pilot named Bill McLaughlin.

Bill told us, "Take it from me, gentlemen, if you learn to fly the T-6, you will never have trouble flying any other aircraft in your career. The Texan is the toughest aircraft to get off the ground and back down safely that you will ever fly."

In retrospect, he was not overstating the truth. The Texan was tricky at low speeds and could stall violently. It would fall off on one wing and jerk into a tight nose-down spiral or spin like a top. It was too much airplane for some of our number. They were quietly reassigned to a base of their choice and sent on their way. I completed the ninety-hour program without a single pink slip, which signified a failed lesson or check ride, and seemed to be at the top of my class in instrument flying.

The Air Force apparently stabilized the pilot corps turnover rate by the end of 1952. However, there were too many potential pilots in the pilot training pipeline. Without prior notice, Southern Airways was directed to identify the lower half of the students according to their academic standing. Within a week, half of Class

54-H were reassigned to the base of their choice and reluctantly left the program.

I was retained for further training and assigned to Laredo AFB, Laredo, Texas, for jet training. The flying was becoming more sophisticated and more fun along each successive step of my training. Our first challenge was to learn formation flying. For this phase we used the T-28 Trojan built by North American Aviation. It was powered by the R-1300-7 engine that developed 800 hp. It had a slight dihedral in the wing that gave it excellent stability in level flight. It had a tricycle landing gear with the main gear wide enough apart to have very little tendency to ground loop. It was a pleasure to fly. Bill McLaughlin was correct to say that future aircraft would be easier to fly than the T-6 Texan.

We flew the Trojan for forty hours and then were introduced to our first jet, the Lockheed T-33 Shooting Star (aka: T-*Bird* or *Converter* since it converted JP-4 jet fuel into noise.) It was easier to fly than the T-28 Trojan! As a jet it had no torque or prop wash that required compensation when taking off and landing. The next ninety hours of training in the T-Bird honed our skills and taught us how to manage the demands of flight at a lightening quick pace. In jet flying, everything happens quickly and the pilots must be sharp and quick to fly them. Getting *behind the aircraft* in timing could lead to deadly consequences.

We had no fatalities during this phase of our training. However, there were some close calls. One pilot was returning from his first solo flight and had a panic attack on his landing approach. He was *high and hot* meaning he was afraid of stalling and crashing on the runway and would not slow the aircraft properly. His instructor was in the small mobile control unit near the approach end of the runway. On the radio he attempted to calm the student and talk him through another approach and landing. The student was higher and faster on the next attempted landing.

After several unsuccessful attempts to convince the student to slow down, the instructor chose a radical tactic. He convinced the student to fly as low as he could to the runway then *stop-cock* the engine. The student agreed. He flew down to about three feet then stopped the engine. However, he was faster than ever. The aircraft settled nicely to the ground and streaked on down the runway. It ran through the overrun, through the perimeter fence, across the highway, through the parking lot of a drive-through and into the dessert beyond. The student was not injured but he resigned from the flying program immediately.

Another incident occurred while I was waiting in the T-Bird queue for takeoff one day. The third aircraft in a lineup of ten students waiting their turn to depart on a solo flight made an unfortunate error in his cockpit checks. The check list suggested while scanning your instruments you *push-to-test* the small instrument lights on each instrument. Just above the *gear up lever* is a guarded red button that should **never, ever** be pushed to test. It is the tip tank jettison button. In an emergency power failure during takeoff that button allows you to jettison the two 200-gallon tanks mounted on the wing tips of the T-Bird. The student, caught up in his ritual of pushing and testing, accidentally jettisoned his tip tanks while in the takeoff queue. The tanks ruptured and 400 gallons of JP-4 jet fuel splashed onto the taxiway.

The mobile control instructor shouted on the radio, "All aircraft awaiting takeoff stop engines immediately! Abandon your aircraft! Run away from the taxiway! This is an emergency! There are 400 gallons of fuel spilled on the taxiway!"

The instructor was rightfully concerned that the jet exhaust would ignite the fuel and the entire line of T-Birds might light up one after the other. I followed the warning without question. Ten of us dashed a hundred yards or so into the grassy median. The fire department arrived promptly and foamed the taxiway surrounding the ill-fated third aircraft. Later, that cadet voluntarily departed the Aviation Cadet Program.

The first eight months of the Aviation Cadet Program were extremely busy. We had very little time for diversion. Therefore, Laredo was a welcomed relief from our tight schedule. We had a Saturday morning fall-out inspection and a barracks inspection. After that we had the prerogative to leave the post if we liked. The base provided a Cadet club for our use. Young women were allowed to enter the post and attend the Cadet Club without sponsor. Saturday and Sunday nights were generally lively at the Cadet Club with plenty of dancing partners to go around. I particularly enjoyed the company of the senoritas. I had taken ten hours of formal training in Spanish at the University of Missouri and enjoyed the opportunity to chat with the Latino girls in their native language.

What a joyful day it was June 24th, 1954, the class of 54-H graduated from flight school. Our commencement speaker was Gill Robb Wilson, editor and publisher of "Flying" magazine. Mr. Wilson was in his nineties. He was slightly palsied. His ancient head shook a bit as he spoke slowly and in a clear voice. He said:

"When I was your age, I thought it had all been done. There was no more adventure to be found in this world. The Civil War was over. My uncle had a mini-ball embedded in his thigh. I couldn't top that. Another uncle ran off to St. Louis with the dancing girl from the pool hall. I couldn't do that either. But then two old boys with a home built airplane taught me to fly. And I have had a lifetime of thrills ever since.

"My generation stood on the shoulders of the Wright brothers who showed the world how to fly. My generation brought forth the jet age and supersonic flight. But, do not think it has all been done. Your generation? Oh, how I wish I could be here to see it. Why, your generation will walk on the moon!"

Jet Fighter Training

With a new silver-tan officer's uniform sporting the gold bars of a second lieutenant and the silver pilot wings, I returned to Kennett for a couple of weeks to be with my mother. Dad had passed on at the early age of 48 due to a rheumatic heart. I know he would have been proud to see me finally flying; though, he would have none of it personally. Dad would drive anywhere in the world, but flying just seemed too risky for him. Mom beamed when I appeared at the door in uniform.

She said, "Oh good, you are here at a perfect time. The Kennett Band is having a concert at the City Park tonight. You can take me and see all of our friends."

What guy doesn't love basking in his mother's pride in front of the people that watched him grow up? The night was one of the most fulfilling nights of my life. My friends and neighbors crowded around me to find out what it is like being a jet pilot.

"How high have you been?"

"How fast does the T-Bird go?"

"Doesn't it take your breath away to loop?"

"Have you been supersonic yet?"

"Can you hear anything when you are going faster than sound?"

Actually, the T-Bird is a trainer and can only fly subsonic. But the aircraft I was to fly in the advanced phase of my training would be supersonic capable. I left Kennett to travel to Valdosta, Georgia, for four months advanced training. Everyone in the class of 54-H wanted a jet fighter assignment. Not all would be assigned to jets. The needs of the Air Force came first. Half of our class was assigned to multi-engine cargo carriers. Five of us who excelled in instrument flying were sent to Valdosta AFB for all-weather training, an intense instrument course to prepare us for Air Defense Command (ADC).

There was no shooting war underway at that time but there was the Cold War. International Ballistic Missiles could reach our shores as well as the long range bombers of our enemy. ADC had the responsibility to detect and meet the threat before the enemy reached our homeland. BOMARC missiles and high altitude interceptors were the backbone of that defense. The interceptor pilots had to be well trained in instrument flying. They had to stand alert and be ready to deploy (scramble) in all weather conditions. I was to be part of the Air Defense Command for the next ten years.

At Valdosta AFB we not only learned to fly instruments to a level of precision I never thought possible, but also how to fly the F-94C Starfire built by Lockheed. This interceptor was equipped with an afterburner for the increased thrust needed to climb rapidly to combat altitude. It was armed with twenty-four Folding Fin Aerial Rockets (FFAR) in the nose of the fuselage and twenty-four more in two pods under the wing. The service ceiling of the Starfire was 51,000 feet but 45,000 feet was a more practical operating altitude.

All jet pilots know that the speed of sound varies with temperature. Lower air temperatures have a slower speed of sound. In fact, in the stratosphere the temperature might be as low as minus 67-degrees Fahrenheit. Under those conditions the speed of sound might be lower than your stall speed. Operating at the top of your aircraft's service ceiling and near your stall speed is known as the *coffin's corner*. Lowering your nose to descend increases your speed. If your aircraft is not designed for supersonic flight, structural damage might occur. The F-94C was a tongue-in-cheek supersonic aircraft. It had a straight wing and did not have a sleek design. It barely had enough power to push through the sound barrier in a dive on a cold day. Part of our training was to fly to 45,000 feet, leave the after burner on and dive vertically through the sound barrier, Mach-1.

The problem was, if the temperature was not cold enough that particular day you might not achieve penetration of the sound barrier. In the transition speed range of Mach-0.98, the pressure waves of the barrier created a low pressure cone that engulfed your elevator. Now, you cannot pull out of the dive by pulling back on the stick. But, if you do nothing, you will continue in the helpless state until you impact the earth. We who flew the F-94C knew that the lack of power to reach the other side of the sound barrier was a design fault. A safe recovery technique was to turn off the afterburner and back away from the transitional speed range to regain elevator control. Once out of the dive there was no further problem with maneuverability at subsonic speeds.

Flying the F-94C was not difficult. But, there were new challenges to become an interceptor pilot. This jet was two placed. A radar observer (RO) rode the back seat. During radar detection and attack of the intruder, the RO gave the pilot steering instructions to position the interceptor into firing position. Keen and prompt coordination between pilot and RO was mandatory for mission accomplishment (MA.)

Second Lieutenant Percival Penn was assigned to me as my RO for the duration of the training at Valdosta. Percy had just completed RO School. They were trained in radar tracking and giving pilots directions while flying in a pair of B-25 aircraft. With several students on board, the B-25s took turns being the intruder and interceptor. A dozen students could be drilled on their techniques on a single four hour mission. However, neither Percy nor any of the RO graduates had ever been in a high altitude interceptor before. On the most part the B-25 flew straight and level. It was my pleasure to indoctrinate Percy into the jet age.

We took our new ROs for an introductory joy ride the first afternoon they arrived. Percy and I blasted off in the F-94C and did a max-performance climb to 45,000 ft. This was our office, up high in the thin air of the stratosphere. I showed Percy that from that altitude we were able to see across the span of Florida. We could see the Atlantic Ocean to the east and the Caribbean Sea to the west. When it was time to return to the base, I rolled inverted and pulled the nose to forty five degrees down to lose half of the 45,000 feet of altitude before leveling off.

I heard Percy comment, "I'm going to have to buy a new hat."

I thought what an odd thing to say after the dazzling ride I had just given him. Later, I became aware that Percy had a slight tendency towards motion sickness. He had used his folding cap as a sickness bag after the inverted descent to a lower altitude. I discovered we were going to have to work on that problem. High altitude intercept work is not straight and level flying. It is high performance flying and that's the fun of it. Percy would have to understand the nature of our work and accommodate to it or find a new job.

Before we graduated from Valdosta, Percy was over the *new guy* nerves and would sit solidly in his seat, reading his radar and giving me directions regardless of the g-load or orientation of our aircraft. He never had to buy another hat.

Chapter 2
Duty Stations

The graduation from Valdosta was without ceremony. We had become all-weather certified and interceptor qualified. We were then scheduled for assignment to our first duty as line pilots. At last, I felt like I had made the varsity team. The class leader held his final group meeting with us. The business of the day was to announce where each of us were to go on our first permanent change of station (PCS.) He read the list of our assignments alphabetically.

"Baker, Elmo C." he barked, "449th Fighter Interceptor Squadron (FIS,) Ladd Air Force Base, Fairbanks, Alaska."

First Permanent Change of Station (PCS)--Alaska

I was stunned--Alaska, the cold country. It was farther north than Goose Bay, Labrador. Why me? I felt like I was one of the best jocks in the class. What's wrong with Tyndall AFB, Florida, or Oxnard AFB, California? The answer became apparent. Those assigned to the frozen station were all single or recently married without children. The far north was difficult duty, bitter cold duty in the winter months. It was no place for small children or large families. We were to spend two years there if we were single; three years if we had a wife. I realized that the Air Force knew best in this case.

I thought, *Perhaps Alaska holds hunting and fishing adventures that will make the hardships worthwhile. Besides, nine of my classmates are going north with me.*

Later that day we were joking about it and discussing what sort of cameras and rifles we were going to take up there with us.

Donald Caskey, a classmate, pulled me aside and confided, "It gets better, Mo. You and I along with Reinhart and Parkhurst are going to Alaska by Military Sea Transportation (MATS)"

"Say what! That can't be right. We are Air Force. We travel by air," I replied.

"Not this time," he affirmed. "It seems that the Army is shipping four hundred soldiers up to Fort Greely by MATS. It's necessary to have a voyage staff for the trip. Parkhurst will be the Commanding Officer; you and I will be Company Commanders, and Reinhart will be the Provost Officer. We join the ship at San Francisco. Then we sail to Seattle to pick up a load of cars. After that we sail four days to Homer, Alaska, to catch a train to Fairbanks. It will be our first command; and it will be fun. Heck! Reinhart will have Court Martial authority. He can throw those doggies in the brig if they don't behave."

After some thought, I agreed with Don. Let's have fun with it. Two weeks later at San Francisco, on October 14, 1956, four Air Force Second Louie's climbed the gangway of a rusty Danish cargo ship under contract to MATs. We were met at the top of the ramp by a six- foot- four Army master sergeant. He snapped to attention and rendered a crisp salute.

He barked, "Welcome aboard, Gentlemen. I am Master Sergeant Wilson. I will be your First Sergeant for this trip. These four soldiers will take your luggage bags to your quarters. Follow me and we will tour the troop bays and mess facilities."

The ship had two cargo holds equipped to sleep 200 soldiers in hammocks stacked three high. The third cargo hold was reserved for the cars we were to pick up in Seattle. Master Sergeant Wilson showed us the mess facilities for the enlisted and the dining room for the captain and officers.

Sailing to Seattle was uneventful and it appeared this trip might be a luxury cruise. At Seattle the third hold was loaded with cars and we departed for Alaska. From Seattle the ship had the option to sail by way of the inside passageway or via the open sea west of all the outer islands. The inside route between the outer islands and the coast of the continent was protected from violent winds and was usually smooth sailing. The open sea route was subject to westerly winds and heavy seas. For some reason the Danish captain choose the open seas, perhaps, because the open sea was easier to navigate; perhaps it was just easier since the inside passage required constant twisting and turning to steer the course; or, perhaps it was just the ancient Viking spirit in our Nordic captain calling him to the open sea.

A day out of Seattle our luxury cruise became a nightmare for the poor soldiers in the holds. High westerly winds and heavy seas tossed the cargo ship violently. At times the pitching was so severe the propellers would be lifted half way out of the water causing a shudder throughout the ship. Huge waves crashed over the bow. All hands and passengers were restricted to below deck. The Army soldiers became horribly sea sick. The passenger holes were awash with vomit for two days and nights.

Fortunately, we four Air Force officers were quartered amidships where the pitching was minimized. As aviators, none of us were sensitive to the ships motion. During the high seas we spent our time together snacking, drinking coffee, playing cards and talking about what adventures might be ahead for us in Fairbanks.

Our final day at sea was calm. The soldiers recovered from their *mal de mar* and were ordered to mop up their mess and prepare for an inspection prior to their disembarkation.

From Homer the slow moving Alaskan Rail Line transported us north. With frequent mail stops, we lumbered through Anchorage, past Denali Park with Mount McKinley, and on to Fairbanks. Several other classmates from Valdosta arrived by air at Fairbanks on the same day.

The Squadron Commander, Major L. E. Dezonia, addressed the new arrivals the following morning. He announced, "You men were selected to join this Squadron because you are current in the F-94C. Unfortunately, we do not have any of those. We were supposed to receive them two years ago to replace their predecessors, our Lockheed F-94 As and Bs.

"That plan has changed. Now the plan is to equip this Squadron with Northrop's F-89D Scorpion this fall. The F-94 As and Bs are being retired to the boneyard at Davis-Mothan AFB in Tucson. You will not have time to learn to fly the As and Bs before they go. We do have three T-33 trainers. You will be flying those until the Scorpions arrive.

"In the meantime, we will give you ground schooling on the F-89D then send all of you to Arctic Survival School to learn how to cope and survive in the frigid north. First Lieutenant Sweeny here will be your Flight Commander and assign you your daily duties-- welcome and good luck. "

First Lieutenant Sweeny was a tall blond-headed guy who appeared to be several years older than we were. Immediately, I wondered what he had done to get stuck in the rank of First Lieutenant. Perhaps he had been an enlisted soldier before going to flight school. He strolled to the front of the briefing room and waited until the CO departed before he spoke.

"You wet-noses are all mine now." He began. "Don't go anywhere or say anything or touch anything without my permission. You will report here every morning at 0730 hours for...."

"Wait a minute!" I interrupted. "What are we going to be doing when we are not flying or in ground school?"

Sweeny slowly turned to face me attempting to intimidate me with a menacing glare. He said, "Who are you?"

"Second Lieutenant Baker, Elmo C., Sir" I responded without the slightest hint of being intimidated.

"Well, Second Lieutenant Baker, Elmo C., Sir, you will be lucky if I don't have you sweeping the floor or cleaning the toilets before I'm through with you," he hissed with clenched teeth.

"Not likely, Sir. I did all that stuff when I was a one-stripper. We are all officers here. We don't pull KP or do menial labor anymore. You better go get yourself some enlisted troops to mop up around here. We are here to fly and fight." I replied without blinking.

Sweeny lifted an eye brow. "You were enlisted?"

"Yep." I didn't mention that I was an enlisted man for only six months while I awaited a slot in the Aviation Cadet program. But during that time I had done my fair share of KP and policing up the cigarette butts from around HQ.

Sweeny smiled and said, "Me too. I like your spirit, Baker. Okay everybody! Here! 0730 hours! We'll get started on your squadron orientation, dismissed."

We didn't have any bullying from Sweeny from then on. My buddies we slapping my back over a beer at the Officer's Club that night. Our Alaskan odyssey was off to a good start.

At 0730 the next day Sweeny found us all seated and eager to get started. He conducted a rather thorough orientation of the squadron and of the base. He took us to the hanger to meet the chief of maintenance and few of the mechanics who would be maintaining the birds we were to fly. He walked us through the underground tunnels that connected the barracks, hangers, Officers Club, movie theater, and all other important buildings on the base. At forty below zero, it is dangerous to trek around above ground.

Before the week was over, we were holding conversations with him about his family and where we were from. As it turns out, the seasoned soldier had a great sense of humor and could relate even the most serious incident with humor.

"Do you guys know that the T-Birds are not being repaired or replaced?" he asked us one day. "They are being sent to the boneyards as they fail. Six months ago one of ours hit the time limit on the engine. I had to take it down to Elmendorf AFB in Anchorage to their boneyard. That was a hoot! Maintenance stripped it of its tip tanks and anything else they could take off of it without endangering my safety of flight. The weather was cloudy but not bad the day I left. I had to get a clearance from Air Traffic Control (ATC) though. I sat on the end of the runway forever waiting for the flight clearance. The fricking T-Bird doesn't fly very long without tip tanks."

He paused, took a breath, made sure he had all of our attention, and then continued, "Finally I got cleared and flew down to Elmendorf but had to enter the holding stack above the clouds because everybody and his dog were trying to get into Elmendorf that day. I watched the fuel gage heading toward empty. So I finally declared a fuel emergency and was told that I was third in line with a fuel- emergency. Damn, if I didn't flame out. The bastard went bone dry while I'm sitting above the clouds at 12,000 feet.

"*Screw it!* I thought.

"We were going to scrap the bird anyway. I wasn't going to 'dead-stick' the bird through the clouds.

"I thought, *Why not just bail out now.*

"I needed to blow the canopy first then fire the ejection seat. I pulled the canopy ejection handle--*nothing!* Maintenance probably grabbed the ejection cartridge when they stripped the bird. So I tried to let the slip stream rip the canopy off by raising it while in flight. That's what the book says to do, doesn't it? The damn canopy went up and sat there like it was on the ramp at home--crap!

"Now, that meant I had to go over the gunnels. I trimmed the T-Bird up to fly straight and level by itself. I unbuckled and stood up. The slip stream slammed me backward into the vertical actuating cylinder that holds the canopy up. Half dazed, I grab the actuating cylinder and found myself flying like a flag on it. I turned loose. Before I could reach the D-ring to open the parachute, it pops open on its own because I'm below 14,000 feet when the aneroid barometer automatically opens the chute. Problem is, I'm in the clouds, blind as a bat and wondering what altitude the bottom of the clouds might be. I dropped through the clouds at maybe 5,000 feet."

Sweeney checked to assure we were all still sucked into his story before he continued, "I was right over Elmendorf! There was busy air traffic all around me. Then, with a big SWOOSH, the T-Bird flies right by me with its canopy open like a crane flying with its mouth open. It had stalled after I left, nosed over and was now gaining speed, which caused it to climb back up into the clouds. I attempted maneuvering the parachute to avoid landing on a runway and getting sucked up someone's intake. I made a little progress when SWOOSH! The damn T-Bird made another pass on me!

"It was trying to kill me for taking it to the bone yard!" Sweeney exclaimed.

"The T-Bird climbed back into the cloud deck. I steered the chute for the bone-yard, which was a mile beyond the end of the operational runway. When I was about 1,000-ft above the ground--SWOOSH! The T-Bird went by me again and planted itself into the bone yard with a crunch. I settle in a few yards away from it. I shucked off the parachute, said my goodbye to the T-Bird, with a few choice expletives, and stomped back towards the base.

"Eventually, a young MP ran toward me with his rifle at high port. He shouted, 'Halt! Halt! Halt! What is the password?'

"I said, 'Shut up! Gather up that parachute back there and follow me.'"

Artic Flying

Fairbanks sits in a topographical bowl, the Matanuska Valley. When September rolls around and the days rapidly get shorter, cold air pools in the Matanuska Valley. The temperature drops to 10 to 20 below zero and the shallow lakes freeze solid. The Arctic Survival School conducted by the Ladd AFB personnel, opens for business. Attendees come from bases all around the world. Twenty of us from the 449th FIS, donned our parkas and mukluks and joined them in the late October class.

After a few days of classroom instructions on the hazards of deep cold, we camped out on the frozen shore of a nearby lake. The first order of the day was to prepare a willow hut for sleeping. We gathered fir boughs and prepared a 3-ft. by 6-ft. pad on the ground that was at least ten inches deep which served to keep our sleeping bag well above the frozen tundra. Then we stuck long willow limbs in the ground six inches apart around three sides of the fir bough pad. We bent the opposing willows into an arch and interlaced them together. Next, we fashioned an interlaced willow entry door. Lastly, we covered the hut with our ponchos and sealed the edges with more fir boughs. Amazingly, a one-inch candle would raise the temperature above freezing inside the hut in a short time. We slept safely and soundly in our sleeping bags and under our parkas. For three days we practiced capturing ptarmigan and trapping snowshoe rabbits.

The senior pilots and ROs ferried the F-94s south that fall and returned with new F-89Ds. It was the first of the year before the junior bird men were transitioned into the big birds. By that time the runways of Ladd AFB were covered with packed snow that made takeoff and landings very tricky.

The squadron commander addressed the new guys saying, "Gentlemen, checking out in a new aircraft is difficult enough in summer weather and on dry runways. You will have to use your best skills to accomplish the transition on snow packed taxiways and runways. Some of you will falter or fail. Do not be ashamed. However, we cannot retain you in this squadron if the challenge is too much for you. We will find you another flying billet here on Ladd AFB that does not evolve taxiing, taking off and landing a war machine on snow loaded runways with 104 folding fin aerial rockets. Good luck to you all."

The CO's prediction came true. Some of the new guys slid off the runway, burying their aircraft in the adjacent snow banks. One hapless pilot was unable to distinguish the taxiway turnoff at the end of the runway. He taxied too far. He went through the overrun and turned onto the perimeter road where he headed for the Officer's Cub. These pilots were allowed to complete their tour at Ladd AFB flying cargo aircraft to deliver supplies to the outposts of the north.

Those of us who qualified to continue flying the big bird soon amassed the fifty hours of proficiency training necessary to enter line duty. Every third day we reported to the Alert Barn at the end of the runway. We stayed there twenty-four hours awaiting the sound of the scramble horn.

Should the horn blow, we raced to the aircraft, started it, and launched for interception of an unknown (bogie) aircraft--all within five minutes. If no launch was ordered during our alert period, we would scramble out of the barn on a training flight early in the morning to allow a fresh pair of aircraft and crew to replace us. The rest of that day was usually down time. The third day of the cycle was ground duty or more proficiency flying. This three-day cycle continued throughout the year without much variation.

When the days of winter were shortened to 3.5 hours, training flights were at a minimum. So the base supplied pastime facilities to keep the morale up. The underground network allowed us to walk to the movies, photo hobby shop, crafts center, auto repair barn etc. Although the weather was bitter, the tour at Ladd AFB was still an adventure.

Wedding Bells and Langley

I joined the chapel choir as a diversion while in Alaska. There I met a beautiful young soprano whose parents, Major Davis and Thelma Newman, were stationed there at Ladd AFB. Merry was a student at Alaska University and the oldest of three daughters. We dated, went to Officer's Club, movies, and house parties for nearly a year. We married in the chapel before I was reassigned to "the Lower 48."

We were assigned to Langley AFB, Virginia, in the summer of 1956. We remained at that station for eight years. We started our family with Melisa and Michael. Merry was active in the Officers' Wives Club, and I pressed hard at my military career by striving to make myself more valuable to the Air Force. Besides my duties as a line pilot, I became the engineering projects officer for the squadron, where I coordinated the efforts of the base engineers to design improvement projects for the squadron facilities and monitored the contractors' construction progress. I attended night school to complete my undergraduate degree. And, through a program called Operation Bootstrap, I attended Syracuse University for the final thirty hours on their campus.

Good Morning, Mr. President

During the eight years in the 48th FIS at Langley AFB I was privileged to fly the best interceptors in the world--first the F-102 Delta Dagger, then the Cadillac of interceptors, the F-106 Delta Dart. The F-106 was a Mach-2 aircraft that could climb to 45,000 feet in 2.5 minutes.

Our mission in the 48th FIS was to protect the Washington D.C. area from intruders into our Air Defense Zone. High altitude threats were met with special techniques. We practiced on U-2 reconnaissance aircraft or other high-flying aircraft of the Air Force. The special technique to reach the intruders higher than our normal service ceiling was to level off at 45,000 feet, accelerate to Mach-1.5 or more, then snap-up to make a front-quarter attack on the intruder just as we were reaching the top of our climb. At that point we were out of both airspeed and the ability to maneuver. We literally fell out of the sky--helpless, without steerage.

This technique caused me some big-time trouble one morning in 1960 just after dawn. After the snap-up, I fell out of the sky from 65,000 feet to 45,000 feet. The big delta wing of the Dart tilted the nose down and the aircraft gathered speed and steerage quickly. The F-106's aerodynamic design was so slick that it fell through the sound barrier on the way down, emitting a massive sonic boom.

The problem was that the White House was located directly below me. They say President John F. Kennedy jumped straight up out of his bed. He immediately grabbed the *red phone* and called the Pentagon Command Post to find out what was happening.

As I recovered from my vertical dive, I turned to the heading for Langley AFB. My training mission was complete. Then suddenly a radio call came from the SAGE Center--the ground radar control.

"Mike Golf 13 is the pilot's name Baker?"

That's odd, I thought. *SAGE never uses the pilot's name and his call sign in the same sentence. It's a security precaution.*

"Affirmative," I responded.

"Mike Golf 13, return to your squadron immediately and contact your OPS officer." SAGE directed.

"Roger, roger--I'm on my way" I said, feeling uneasy about it.

The flight from DC to Langley AFB was a ten minute flight for the F-106. Arriving at home base I parked, dismounted the bird, and hiked into the operations office. Major Jim Martin, the Operations Officer, had a telephone receiver in his hand and a frown on his face.

He transferred the phone to my hand as he spoke, "Here, Baker, you talk to this guy!"

It was a major general who was manning the Pentagon Command Post. Sternly he queried, "Captain Baker, can you tell me why you boomed the White House this morning? I have to give the President a damn good reason for your actions."

During my ten-minute flight from DC to Langley AFB I had rehearsed my explanation.

"Sir," I began with all the confidence I could muster, "The mission of the 48th FIS is to protect the White House from all aerial attacks including ultra-high flying intruders. To do this we must fly higher than our service ceiling with a snap-up maneuver. We practice this on every ultra-high target flying over the DC area that we can, even in pre-dawn hours. Following the snap-up we fall helplessly out of the sky having expended all our speed to reach the target. Our aircraft falls into a steep dive on its own and goes supersonic in the process. As soon as we are able to regain control we pull out of the dive and return to base to rearm. Please, convey my apologies to the President for startling his family but we practice this extremely difficult maneuver to protect them."

The General replied, "Hmm, seems like a lot of bullshit to me, Baker. But I'll tell him what you said."

Shortly thereafter, there was a *Notice to All Airman* (NOTAM) posted on all air bases stating that from this day forward there will be a circular area of thirty-mile radius around the White House in which all training flights will be prohibited. If I'm not mistaken, that order exists to this day.

The Cuban Missile Crisis

The 48th Fighter Interceptor Squadron (FIS), under the command of Lieutenant Colonel Jimmy Jumper, who later achieved the rank of lieutenant general, was deployed to Patrick AFB, Florida, during the 1962 Cuban Missile Crisis. With the help of the

USSR, Cuba was constructing surface-to-air missile (SAM) sites on the island. The action was a brazen act of intimidation and a serious threat to the national security of the United States. To permit enemy missiles to be located ninety miles from American soil was unthinkable and could not be tolerated. Naturally, President Kennedy was adamantly opposed to the Soviet maneuver to intimidate the US.

The 48th FIS set up shop on the median of the runways with three trailers. Our F-106s were lined up on a taxiway ready to scramble on any flying threat emanating from Cuba. To get closer to the threat, we flew round-the-clock combat air patrols with two aircraft in a race-track orbit thirty miles off shore from Havana. Pilots were on duty twenty-four hours and off duty twenty-four hours for the duration of the crisis. It was exciting to stand nose-to-nose with an enemy. Those of us who flew twenty combat air patrols or more received an Air Medal citation for our vigilance. I was proud to be on the varsity team in an actual threat environment.

Prequel to Vietnam

Interceptors are heavily equipped with electronic gear to operate the aircraft, utilize the radar for target detection, and tracking, as well as for combating the target's attempt at electronic counter measures. The sophisticated gear piqued my interest in electronics. The Air Force Institute of Technology (AFIT) at Wright-Paterson AFB at Dayton, Ohio, needed good candidates for Electronic Engineering training. Since I had graduated Cum Laude from Syracuse University — class of 1965. I was selected to attend AFIT. It was a great honor to join a class of twenty other captains who were selected for their academic achievements. The next two years were among the busiest I have ever experienced. The studies were intense and relentless. I studied until two o'clock a.m. every night.

Merry and the children had my company all day Sunday. During the week days we shared the evening meal and very little time other than that. I studied into the wee hours of the mornings. In the end, the hard work paid off. I graduated with honors and was promoted to major. After twelve years in the service, I felt that I had a solid role in the Air Force and was prepared for greater responsibilities and challenges.

Before I left AFIT, the head of the engineering department, Doctor Zieman, called me into his office for a chat.

Zieman said, "Congratulations, Major Baker, on your achievements here. You graduated with honors and have been inducted into the Engineering Honor Society, Etta Kappa Nu. You were promoted to major as well. I personally want to thank you for serving as president of the students' chapter of Industrial Electronics and Electrical Engineers (IEEE.) And, I appreciate you developing the computer program for me to describe the 'E'-field within a wave guide. It's the first of its kind in this Institute and I have made it part of our collection of *Advance Programs for Electronic Engineers.*

"I understand that you must join the war effort before you continue your career in electronics. After your F-105 training and 100 missions in Vietnam, you will be welcome here on my staff of instructors if you so choose."

There was never the thought I would not finish my 100th mission over Vietnam. There was always that possibility, but it was never a part of my plan for the future.

Merry and I packed up and with the kids moved to McConnell AFB, Wichita, Kansas. We rented a small house near the elementary school we liked and settled in for the fall and winter of 1966. I was assigned to one of the three training squadrons that had the responsibility to train F-105 pilots to be sent to Takhli or Korat, Thailand, in order to fly deep strikes into North Vietnam. All of the instructors and even some of the aircraft had actually been to combat in Vietnam. I joined five other majors and sixteen captains in training at the 561st Tactical Fighter Squadron commanded by Lieutenant Colonel L.E. McKenny. I couldn't wait to get my hands on the F-105.

The Republic F-105 Thunderchief "Thud" was the largest fighter-bomber built to that date. It was a Mach-2 bird with a huge Pratt & Whitney J-75 engine. Fully loaded with armament and fuel it had a gross weight of over 50,000 pounds. Its bomb load exceeded the famous B-17 Flying Fortress of WWII days. Republic designed the Thud for the Cold War. It was to stand alert in case of a nuclear exchange between the USSR and the NATO nations. It had the ability to dash low-level at supersonic speeds below the enemy radar and strike Russian targets with a nuclear weapon.

It was never required to strike during the Cold War. However, it was a marvelous fighter-bomber for interdiction into North Vietnam. It could carry a three-thousand pound bomb under each wing, each capable of creating a crater 125 feet in diameter. It also had the most astonishing Gatling gun, the M-61, six barrel 20mm gun that fired 6000 rounds per minute. That's 100 rounds per second! The rounds were essentially following each other nose to tail. Each round can blow a bushel basket size hole in reinforced concrete. Such fire power could cut a pontoon bridge in half like a buzz saw.

My first duty at the 561st TFS was to study the systems of the F-105, the operating procedures, and the emergency actions. Ground school was meticulous and extensive. The Thud was big, sophisticated, and unforgiving to mishandling or mismanagement. I felt like I was now playing on the first team of the American fighting force.

While I poured over the flight manual day and night, Merry concentrated on introducing the children to their new elementary school. Merry was a fine seamstress and dressed the children in bright, stylish attire. One night a few weeks into the new school year, my daughter Melisa knocked on my study room door.

"Daddy, may I talk to you about something?" Melisa asked.

"Sure, Sugar Babe. What is it?"

"I feel out" she said

"Feel out what? " I replied.

"At school, I feel out, not in" she complained.

"Oh, why is that?"

"Because mother sends me to school in pretty dresses every day and none of the other girls dress like that" she explained

"I see. How do they dress?" I wondered.

"They wear dresses from K-Mart and are not afraid of getting dirty or messed up. I want to wear plain dresses to school too," she said.

"Well, I can fix that. "I promised.

That weekend, the family shopped the K-Mart store and from then on the kids felt part of the crowd at school.

Soon I completed the ground school. Then one day, the 21st of November, 1966, I stepped into my new office, the cockpit of the mighty F-105D Thunderchief "Thud." She fired up with easy grace and stood gently waiting while I ran a few checks to determine her health and readiness. A check list of procedures was strapped to my left thigh. I scanned the seventy-five instruments mounted on the panels before me. They looked good to me.

"Red Flight, check in," came the radio call from Captain Jack Redman, my flight instructor.

"Red two is on," I replied.

"Roger--McConnell tower, Red Flight with two ready to taxi," he called.

The tower cleared us to taxi. I flipped my thumbs outward to the crew chief. He pulled the chocks and I nudged the Thud forward about a foot and taped the brakes for a functional check. Then I let her slowly roll forward and fall in trail with Red One.

Fighter pilot wives say their husbands are in love with their aircraft. They say she is his mistress. It is probably true. I dearly loved the F-102 and the F-106. Now I was getting pretty excited about the F-105. On our way to the runway the Thud moved like silk down the taxiway.

I think she whispered to me, *Mo, we will be great together. I am yours. I will do anything you tell me to do.*

When Red Flight took the active runway we paused abreast. Jack swirled his index finger in the air to wind them up. I pushed my throttle forward. As 14,000 pounds of hot thrust poured from the tailpipe, the nose dipped a bit. She was a racehorse in the gate, waiting to be released. I checked my engine instruments: RPM, EGT, Fuel Flow, Oil Pressure, etc. All okay. I gave jack a nod and he was rolling. Thirty seconds later I followed. The Thud was eager to go. She wanted to show me what she could do. Our romance had begun.

In the preflight briefing earlier Jack had told me he was glad to have a student who had flown high performance jets before. He did not have to start from scratch with me. The F-106 and the F-105 have the same J-75 engine. They were both powerful machines that were top of the line. Since Jack had demonstrated the basic stall characteristics to me in the two-place version, the F-105F, a few days before, the solo ride that day was going to be a full performance demonstration to show me the Thud's capabilities and build my confidence in her.

After clearing the control zone around McConnell AFB we dropped to five hundred feet and pushed the throttle up to 500 knots. The Thud was built for this. She was stable and sure-footed. She responded to my slightest touch as if she were reading my mind.

Jack put me in trail three hundred yards and whistled across the Kansas plains, weaving and turning in long, graceful arcs. The Thud wasn't even breathing heavy.

She spoke to me, *You see Mo, I told you we were going to be great together. And, I have a lot more to show you yet.*

Without notice Jack pulled the stick back, lit the after burner, and shot skyward in a near vertical climb to 25,000 feet. Then rolled over on his back and pulled the nose down into a forty five degree dive. The Thuds stuck together as if they were tethered. She was really showing off for me now. We leveled at 500 feet again and continued to dissect Kansas in tandem.

Suddenly, Jack did a rapid aileron roll to the left but stopped the roll three quarters around and sucked the Thud into a four-g turn to the right. This maneuver was a technique to shake off a follower and escape to the right. My gal was not fooled. We duplicated the three-quarter roll and pulled gracefully into trail of Jack's turn. She followed the twin vapor trails spinning off Jack's wing tips effortlessly.

After his wide turn we took up a heading for home. Jack waggled his wings and I joined up. Together we returned to McConnell AFB. The crew chiefs met us with a crisp salute, put the wheel chocks in place, and called for engine shut off with a finger cut motion across his throat.

Before I shut down the engine, I thought I heard her say, *I told you we were going to be good together. I can't wait to do this again.*

A crew van picked us up and offered us a cold wet towel as we returned to the readiness room.

"What do you think?" Jack asked, knowing the answer.

"I'm hooked, I'm smitten, and I'm in love!" I grinned.

The next three months were busy with developing our skills on strafing, bombing, firing rockets, shooting a towed banner, and air-to-air refueling. Another facet of our training was low level navigation using the radar ground mapping returns. At 500 feet and 400 knots we could stay below the enemy radar but had to rely on the radar to detect land features to steer the course. Grain silos and water towers were convenient objects for good radar returns.

Ponds and lakes absorb radar energy and appear as black holes on the radar. They too are excellent checkmarks for low level operations. However, ducks on the water are a real hazard if they are spooked into flying. I was amazed at how well we could navigate if we carefully monitored our estimated time between check points and looked for our land features.

Twenty-two pilots were in the Replacement Training Unit (RTU) at the 561st. All were volunteers and unafraid of the dangerous flying tasks they would face in the combat zone. They were there to prepare for battle. The class of twenty-two was typical. It contained a mix of seasoned military men with obvious talent for flying as well as some junior birdmen that were willing but novice warriors. Some of these men had distinguished combat tours and went on to very successful military careers.

One of the most notable in our group was John Piowaty, a strong individualist that wore a handle bar mustache to show his stance among the many. John was formerly an enlisted troop. He was a survival instructor at Stead AFB prior to entering flight school. John was a natural pilot. And he was a meticulous records keeper. To this day he has the flight planning card of every mission he has flown in his life.

Bruce Stocks was wise beyond his years. He went to battle as a *Wild Weasel* flying the two-placed version of the F-105 with a weapons officer in the back seat. Their mission was to fly far out in front of the larger strike force alone to detect SAM sites and suppress their abilities to attack the fighter-bombers.

Our top-gun was Captain Phillip Drew, a handsome, intelligent warrior who already had a 100 mission tour in the back seat of an F-4 Phantom jet in South Vietnam. Phil completed his 100 missions in North Vietnam as a Wild Weasel and went on to a successful military career, retiring as a brigadier general.

Then there was a threesome of note; Pete Lane, Chet Griffin, and Criss Lawrence. These men were super pilots that could really

32

stir the stick. Their natural talent caused the Operations Officer, Captain John Shay, to comment, "Those guys don't know how good they actually are. They can fly the Thud and probably the box it came in."

And then there was me, the only guy in the class photos that was actually smiling. Obviously, I was having the time of my life. I was *self-actualizing.* I was doing what I believed Mo Baker was put on this earth to do.

"Flying jets is dangerous even without enemy Triple-A or anti-aircraft artillery fire," affirmed John Shay the Ops Officer earlier in our check-out training. "There may be fatal mistakes during your training. Hurling yourself and a 50,000 pound aircraft at the ground in order to place a free falling bomb or rocket on a target will inevitably take its toll."

And so it was. One of our class members who had limited experience in high-performance jets followed his rockets into ground with *target fixation.* Sadly, the class of 22 graduated without one of its members. Fortunately, the remaining aviators in the class returned from their combat duty in Vietnam with the exception of one who was shot down on his sixty-second mission over North Vietnam — me.

With about 3,000 hours of flying time, most of it in jets, I felt that I was ready for combat duty. After a raucous party to say goodbye to the 561st TFS and their great instructors, Merry and I packed up and moved to San Antonio, Texas, with the kids to be near her parents and her high school friendship group.

Working My Way to Southeast Asia

I took thirty days leave after Requalification Training Unit (RTU) in order to relocate the family to San Antonio and have a proper vacation before leaving for South East Asia. We found a cute three-two brick in Inspiration Hills. Merry had a few minor modifications for me to make--namely to convert the garage into a

TV-Entertainment room. There was still time for a family trip to Laredo to visit Old Mexico before I left.

There were three brave faces saying goodbye to me at the airport the day I left. Military wives and children are accustomed to their guy going away for temporary duty from time to time. But this time, we were all aware of the danger involved and the real possibility that we may never meet again. To her credit, Merry never said a word to discourage me from going. She knew this was my moment in history. She knew I wanted to fulfill the appointment. She knew not only did I have to fulfill my duty but I was eager to go. This is what fighter pilots and other warriors do. They are compelled to go into battle. It is their chosen destiny.

The first stop on the way to the battlefields was Clark AFB in the Philippine Islands. Jungle Survival School, aka *Snake School*, was mandatory training for all military members going to Southeast Asia. I was thrilled at the opportunity to complete another survival school. While growing up in Missouri, my father had served the Boy Scouts of America (BSA) as District Commissioner. He visited every church and civic club in the region to solicit sponsors for Boy Scout troops. I was his poster boy. From the age of twelve I would go with him on the solicitations and say my little speech about the origin and history of BSA. Troop weekend camp outs, Jamborees, and summer scout camps were a way of life for me.

By the time I graduated from high school I had experienced hundreds of nights in the wilderness. For this reason I volunteered for survival schools in the military. They were like bigger and better BSA camp-outs. By this time in the military, I had already attended Arctic Survival at Ladd AFB, Alaska, Deep Sea Survival at Langley AFB, Virginia, and Worldwide Survival at Fairchild AFB, Washington.

Jungle survival was vital to Southeast Asia duty. After one week of ground school to identify the jungles hazards and how to avoid them such as panthers, venomous snakes and monstrous boa constrictors (they actually had a sixteen-foot boa in captivity there to show us. They called him Ralph and fed him a live duck each week.) They schooled us in what food was available and prepared some of it for us in class. We sampled snake and fried grass hoppers for example.

"You can eat anything that walks, crawls, slithers or flies, if you boil it," said Sgt. Hicks, our survival instructor. "Just make sure you are the eater and not the eatee."

Finding water was simple. I had already learned in Scout camp that a hanging vine an inch or more in diameter was a grand source of water. Simply cut a four foot section, lift vertically over your mouth and let the sap drip or run in. When the flow of the watery sap stopped it was because the capillaries of the upper part of the vine had closed. Cut off six inches of the upper part of the vine and continue. When traveling, strap a few sections of vine to your back as a portable water source.

The next week of Jungle survival was spent in the Jungle, learning to find food and to build a sleeping pad in the trees like the monkeys do. These skills were taught to us by the Negritos or Pygmies. These four-foot tall black people were natives of the jungles and, pound-for-pound, were the strongest people I've ever seen. They are skilled trackers and feared warriors. It was told that the Japanese attempted to occupy their territories during WWII only to lose many soldiers in the night. The Japanese moved away from the Negritos because they could neither find nor confront them.

Sgt. Hicks, our field instructor, related an interesting illustration of why the survival school placed such value on Negrito assistance in our training. He related that a couple of decades ago, the Negrito chief approached the commandant of the Jungle Survival School with a proposal.

He said, "You need to use my men as your perimeter guards and assistant field instructors."

The commandant said, "We are well manned in those areas and have no requirement for additional instructors."

"You are not as well manned as you think. Let's run a test on your night guards that patrol the perimeter of your compound." said the Chief.

"What test?"

"You'll see. Before you relieve them from duty in the morning, have them line up in front of your office for inspection," said the Chief.

The Commandant agreed and shortly after dawn the perimeter guards were in rank before the Commandant's office.

The Negrito Chief said, "Ask them to report if anything unusual was seen last night."

Nothing was reported.

"Now, inspect the inside of their boot heels," said the Chief.

The inspection revealed a small chalk mark on the inside of one heel of each guard. Sgt. Hicks said the Negritos have been on a security duty contract ever since.

As part of our practical escape and evasion training, we were to attempt to practice escape and evasion into the jungle, camp overnight, and return to the base camp by noon the following day. We were to evade in pairs and all given three hours head start before the Negritos started tracking us. Each pair of evaders carried with them three white wooden discs the size of coffee can lids. Should a Negrito tracker discover us, we were to give him a disc that he later redeemed for a pound of rice at the Jungle School Headquarters.

I was assigned an evader mate who had never camped out a day in his life. He was a flight surgeon who had just finished college and had only been in the Air Force a few months. We had a lot of fun although the doctor was fairly spooked about being in the jungle. The evaders launched at noon. I navigated to obvious check points so I could find our way back. Not to make it too easy on the tracker, I backtracked several times to make a ninety degree change in heading to another promontory.

The Doc and I tucked ourselves in by three p.m. well off the paths and completely out of sight. In two hours we were found. We relocated and were promptly exposed again. The third time we were discovered in an even shorter time. The Negritos knew that jungle like the back of their hand.

As dark was approaching and we no longer had an obligation to hide, we selected a ridge top to make our bed and watch the stars. Around nine in the evening we heard the patter of little feet. A Negrito hunter ran up to our camp with a grin on his face. He was half naked and was not one of the Jungle Survival School contract trackers.

"Are we in danger?" ask the Doc.

"I don't think so. From my vast experience with National Geographic magazines, I understand they are not taking heads anymore. They do like American cigarettes, however. I have some with me for this very reason." I said.

I pulled out a pack of cigarettes and offered Negrito one. He accepted and squatted down to await a light. Neither the doc nor I smoked but we all lit up with our new buddy. He puffed hardily. In between puffs he talked. Pointing to the moon he said;

" Suma Negrito, *umbac*."

'Suma American, *moon*" I said.

"Ah, *moon, moon, moon*," he said.

Through the time it took to smoke a second cigarette we enjoyed a point and talk language lesson. After which he stood up and banished a Japanese bayonet saying, "Nipponese." Then he drew the blade across his throat. I suppose that was the way he obtained the blade. With a toothy grin he turned and trotted off into the dark toward home.

The doc looked at me and said, "Whew, now that was different."

We slept soundly until dawn. Then we made our way back out of the Jungles of the Philippines. Sgt. Hicks met us and informed us that none of us had successfully escaped and evaded the Negritos. However, since we were new at it and they were perhaps the best trackers in the world, we all graduated and received our Jungle Survival School Certificate.

Back at Clark AFB we learned that the C-130 cargo ship that normally transported the graduates of the Jungle Survival School from Clark AFB to Bangkok, Thailand, for connections to their squadron assignments was overbooked. So the Doc, I, and several others had the weekend to visit Manila and see the bright lights. We rented a car from the base facility and drove to Manila through the quaint villages and towns, stopping on the way to see points of interests. We selected a tourist approved hotel and asked the bell captain where should we start first to enjoy the Manila mystique.

"I will arrange an escort for you to prevent you from stumbling into a bad neighborhood. He will have a suitable vehicle." The bell captain explained, "Your rental has a government license plate and invites mischief. Your escort works for tips and a small commission from the establishments you visit"

A twenty-year-old Filipino named Rudy appeared promptly at our door. He recommended a restaurant serving typical Island cuisine and pleasant atmosphere. We followed that experience with a live musical and after diner drinks. But, before returning to the hotel, we insisted on Rudy showing us where the locals go for their late night entertainment. The Doc and I tapered off of an evening of good food, music, and libation with a couple of Singha beers while watching beautiful island girls and their guys dancing. It was a wonderful pause in our trek to the combat zone.

Back at Clark AFB, I met Pete Lane and Chet Griffin who had troubling news for me.

Pete explained, "We are not going to Bangkok tomorrow, Mo. We three are being called to Japan to join a program called *Ryan's Raiders*. It seems that General Ryan is not pleased with the fact that we are fighting a war without an all-weather capability. We are flying daytime missions and only in fair weather. He wants to be able to strike North Vietnam at night or in the weather if the mission requires it."

I said, "So?"

Chet answered, "So, we are all-weather pilots with a thousand hours each flying single seated Century Series aircraft with one hand and running the radar with the other hand. We are his kind of boys. He says the enemy is getting too much relaxation at night and during rainy days. He wants us to go low-level under their radar cover into North Vietnam at night alone without all the jamming support aircraft and hassle the Hanoi area."

"Hassle? I want to be a strike pilot not a hassle pilot," I said.

"Ours is not to reason why. Ours is but to do or die," Chet muttered.

The next day, a C-130 flew us up to Itzuke AFB, Japan. Reluctantly, the following morning we found our way to the training facility which was to explain the hush-hush program and convert us into hassle pilots. The Officer-In-Charge of training met us with a round of hot coffee.

"Guys, your training is on hold for about a week," he said, "We have already trained three crews. They're in-country now, (meaning on-station at Takhli, Royal Thai Air Base [RTAB,] Thailand.) They will run a few missions to prove the concept and tweak the tactics. Then we will tune you guys up to join them. So take a week off to see Tokyo. Keep in touch and report back here next Monday."

"Party Time!" we said.

If we were going to die, we may as well have a smile on our face. Back at the Visitor's Quarters we quickly made plans to catch the commuter train into Tokyo and start the party. Over the next four days we took the *Golden Tour of Ginza*, prowled the parks and bars, as well as learned what a Hotsi bath was. We generally burned off all the travel money we had in our pockets. When checking in the fifth day we were called down to the training squadron. The news was grim.

The training officer said, "Suit up, boys; you are on the way to Takhli Royal Thai Air Base, Thailand, tomorrow. The *Ryan's Raiders* program has been canceled. The three crews in-country were all lost. No details on how they went down yet. Probably the low-level inbound run over the hilly terrain at night wiped them out. Tragic! You guys are assigned to separate strike squadrons at Takhli RTAB. Your orders are ready now--good luck."

After months of anticipation, we were finally getting into the fray. At Takhli RTAB the next day, I picked up the base phone at the Base Operations Reception Center and dialed the 357th Tactical Fighter Squadron Operations office. The duty officer answered.

I said, "This is Major Baker, It has taken forever to get here but if you still need me, I'm here at the reception center and ready to do battle."

"Super! Damn right we need you, Baker. I'll send a driver to pick you up," he replied.

I stepped outside on the runway side of the Base Operations Reception Center to wait for the driver and took a deep breath. It was May 10, 1967. I breathed deeply and savored the tropical air, rich in aromas of the lush flora as well as the JP-4 fuel exhausts of jet aircraft taxiing and taking off on the missions of the day.

I thought, *at last I am here. I am here to do what I was born to do.*

Chapter 3
COMBAT OVER VIETNAM

The Vietnam War was not a popular war. The US forces were thrust into battle without the popular support that other servicemen enjoyed. But, military men do not debate the morality of war. They rely on civilians to do that. Military men train for war, practice for war, and wait for the moment when the Commander-in-chief calls for them to perform.

I was not reluctant to fly and fight in Vietnam. It was my profession, my duty, and the thing I had trained to do for over ten years.

357th Tactical Fighter Squadron

As an F-105D strike pilot I arrived at the 357th Tactical Fighter Squadron (TFS) at Takhli, Thailand, in May of 1967. The squadron had lost nearly half of its pilots the previous three months. With 3,000 hours of fighter time and twenty combat missions over Havana in 1962, I felt well trained and eager to join the fray. Because I held the rank of major I became the senior flight commander of the 357th TFS. I flew as Force Commander or Deputy Force Commander each time our squadron led the gaggle.

Thirty-one of my sixty-one missions were in Route Pack Six, the Hanoi area, *downtown* as we called it, where the varsity players meet and greet. Hanoi was one of the most lethally defended cities in all of history. There were MiGs, SAMs, and every rapid-firing anti-aircraft in the communist arsenal.

Lieutenant Colonel Ben Murph was the Commander of the 357th Tactical Fighter Squadron of the 355th Tactical Fighter Wing commanded by Colonel Robert Scott. Murph and I were old friends from the 48th FIS at Langley where he served as the Senior Flight Commander, the third highest position in the squadron.

A competent and serious minded career officer, he was not without a sense of humor. While serving at Langley, Ben and his next senior flight commander, Captain A.B. Hennehan, often played practical jokes on one another. One Christmas their boss, Ops Officer Major Jim Martin, announced that he was taking two weeks leave over Christmas and New Year's. While he was gone one of them must man the Ops Office for a week at a time. They could flip a coin to see who stays at the office Christmas week. Murph won the toss.

So while he was on leave, Hennehan went into his quarters and ran his bath tub full of hot water and stirred in pounds of Jell-O powder. It was the GI-type Jell-O that takes on a sturdy, rubbery consistency and never melts at room temperature. With a can of Cool Whip he wrote *Merry Christmas* on the top of the green monolith.

Returning home from a long road trip, dog tired, the Murph family had to dig out thirty gallons of Jell-O before they could scrub up the kids and tuck them in for the night. Murph was not to be out done. While Hennehan was on his leave over the New Year's holiday, Murph ran an ad in the base newspaper saying "I need your old Christmas tree for my chipper. Just drop it on my front lawn at 124 C Street." Hennehan, who did not own a chipper, returned from his leave to a hundred dried Christmas Trees covering his front lawn.

As I walked into the 357 TFS the memories of our days at Langley were fresh in my mind as Murph grabbed my hand in a firm shake and welcome me to Southeast Asia.

He said, "We need you here, Mo. We have had some losses the last four months. All of them were good men. The activity has been intense. The MiGs have taken a break for retraining lately, but the anti-aircraft artillery and surface to air missiles (SAM) have been brutal.

"You will be the Senior Flight Commander and Major Tom Moore will be your Ops Officer. I am finished with my tour and on my way out of here. I believe Lieutenant Colonel Obadiah Dugan will be your Squadron CO."

"I understand," I said. "When do I get started?"

"Well, you will not be going into Route Pack Six, the Hanoi area, until we can get a few sorties on you in the lower Route Packs. Once we feel you are comfortable being shot at, we will send you up North as a wingman where the varsity anti-aircraft gunners are. Not to worry--You'll get there soon enough. Tomorrow you and Tom Moore will go local as a two-ship to see the area and learn the topography."

Vietnam is shaped like a large letter S. The principle cities of North Vietnam were Hanoi and Haiphong. The principle cities in the South were Saigon and Hue. For targeting purposes, North Vietnam was divided into six areas called Route Packages or RPs.

Murph introduced me to the staff and other jocks that were in the building. He explained that the Royal Thai Air Base of Takhli had one runway that was nearly 10,000 feet long. However the parallel taxiway served as a runway when the main runway was obstructed for some reason. The base was secure and fairly distant from the enemy. We had a fine Officer's Club with bar and restaurant.

He cautioned, "The Thai girls waiting tables at the O-Club are children of the Thai Officers across the base. They are off-limits. They are cute but untouchable. The Wing Commander is adamant about this. Besides, they are children only 15-18 years of age. On the other hand, there is a nice village just outside the base that has two or three bars complete with professional women. Prostitution is not illegal here. However, gonorrhea is a problem so be careful out there."

The US Forces had maintained a presence at the Takhli RTAB for over two years though they choose not to publicize it to the media. At first the crew quarters were hard-sided tents on stilts. Gradually those were replaced with twelve-man frame buildings with window air conditioners. I was assigned to one of the new quarters and found myself with eleven junior birdmen as roommates. We had a common area with a kitchenette, bar, and poker table. The bar was stocked with the best booze one could buy in the country.

We each contributed to the kitty to keep beer, booze, and snacks in stock. The feeling among the warriors was that since life is so tenuous in the combat zone, you may as well have the best life has to offer while you are here. Two house girls, La-ong and Anong, cleaned daily, washed our flight suits, and polished our flight boots.

The following morning I was invited to the Wing Commanders office to meet the boss. Colonel Robert Scott explained our mission.

He said, "Our Wing is tasked to fly 1500 sorties per month. We have three Squadrons, each with 24 or 25 aircraft. That means each aircraft will fly 20 times per month. Actually, with maintenance and inspections taking a few out of action each day, some of the birds fly every day. The more we fly the Thud the more reliable it becomes. We have a larger number of aircrew than aircraft, so you will be flying every other day or so. I won't lie. The missions are dangerous and some of us will not reach the 100 mission goal that allows us to rotate back to the States. Good luck to you and God Speed."

That afternoon, Major Moore and I fired up a couple of Thuds for a two-hour orientation sortie. Thailand is the *Rice Bowl of Indochina* because of its vast expanse of flat, fertile land which is the Mekong River delta. The expanse is interrupted here and there by a vertical, flat-topped, 200 foot hill known as a Karst. Low level high speed flyers must be aware of these sudden outcrops. The orientation gave me a deep sense of the dependency the rural people have on the success of the rice crops they grow each year.

I witnessed thousands of peasants bent over their fields tending their rice paddies. Their homes were thatched roofed houses of teak wood on eight foot stilts nestled around a twenty foot wide pond that served them all as a water source and bathing facility. Later when I visited some of these homes, I found the peasants to be happy people and very family oriented. The entire family slept in one common bed. Little children remained naked from the waist down until they were five or six years old. Beneath the raised house the families raised chickens and pigs.

Their primary diet was rice with vegetables and small portions of pork, fish, or poultry. Garlic seemed to be a favorite seasoning. Peasant fathers usually had one wife. However, as the family income rose it was common to have additional wives depending upon the level of affluence.

The next few days were spent visiting the headquarters, attending mission debriefings, touring the tower and mobile control facilities, and observing the armament teams loading and unloading the aircraft with the different ordnance sets. The Thud carried six 750 pound bombs, M117s, on a multiple ejection rack (MER) mounted on the centerline of the belly. Alternatively, the Thud could carry two 3000 pound bombs, M118s, under each wing with a 600 gallon fuel tank on the centerline belly mounts. Additionally, two *Sidewinder* heat seeking missiles were attached on the outboard stations. Internally, the aircraft always flew with 1020 rounds of 20mm ammunition for its M61 Gatling gun. The Thud was a consummate fighting machine.

The next day Major Moore took me on an actual combat mission. It was to Route Pack One (RP-1) just north of the ten-mile wide demarcation zone that divided North Vietnam from South Vietnam. This Demilitarized Zone (DMZ) was closely guarded by each contender in the war to avoid infiltration. RP-1 was a mostly rural area and had very little anti-aircraft or SAM defense and no MiGs. It served as a training ground for new comers to the conflict.

We flew into enemy territory looking for convoys or suspected truck parks. We saw nothing so we dropped our 750s on what looked like earthen works near the DMZ. Upon returning to the base as a matter of standard operating procedure, we debriefed with the intelligence guys and reviewed our combat film of the mission. To my surprise, my film showed that a lone anti-aircraft gunner had shot at me without success. Little puffs of flack had followed me in on my bomb drop. I was now a combat pilot.

Rules of Engagement

I was ready to do the thing I was trained to do: fly in combat against an enemy. However, the warriors flying strike missions over North Vietnam were never released to fight at their full potential. We could spar with the opponent but were restricted from delivering a blow which could knock him out. Our *Rules of Engagement*, given to us by the generals in the Pentagon, dictated how we could fight. History has revealed to the world that they, the generals, were further restricted by a totally controlling and often self-defeating administration in the Lyndon Johnson White House.

Secretary of Defense Robert McNamara and President Johnson controlled the airstrikes against the enemy targets. They chose what was to be a target and what was off limits. As I made ready to fly over Hanoi and take my attack to the enemy, it would be on targets that they alone selected. That is an odd way to ever fight a war.

We did not have the right or authority in the field--nor did the Joint Chiefs of Staff have the authority to choose, designate, and target locations in Vietnam and call for actions or strikes. Target selection went past the Joint Chiefs of Staff into the Department of

Defense. McNamara and LBJ debated every target. We received word back through some late shoot-down that LBJ had said, "Them boys can't bomb an outhouse without my permission."

We could only hit designated targets. Those came to us in what was called a Frag order, which is Fragmentary Order which only dictated our part in the battle order of the day. We would get a Frag order for the morning strike at sometime around 1600 or 1700 hours the evening before. We would develop our plans that evening for the morning strikes. Afternoon strikes were developed from Frags received by 0900 hours in the morning. For the morning strikes we'd get our flight plan in and look at the weather, prepare our briefing and bomb load. By daybreak we'd have everybody briefed. The timing was usually to place us on the target in North Vietnam sometime around 8:00 AM, plus or minus fifteen minutes. The North Vietnamese could practically set their clocks by us. But, the strike was going to be on an approved target which we had struck before and again and again.

It turned out the Air Force was severely affected by that practice. A photo reconnaissance airplane flying up and down the northeast railroad, taking pictures, and looking for a supply train coming down from China could take its picture. It could send it off to the Department of Defense, McNamara's office and his analyst. The Air Force pilots in Vietnam could ask to strike this train which was sitting under a tree in the daytime, because it moved a night. It took thirteen hours to get an answer back to that pilot circling overhead, giving him authorization to make the strike. By that time, the train was already down the track to Hanoi. Also, the aircraft and pilot would have long since returned to the base. A train doesn't take thirteen hours to drive to Hanoi. The target opportunity was therefore lost due to the naivety of LBJ and McNamara's leadership.

There was no such thing as attacking targets of opportunity in Route Pack-6, the dangerous area north of the Red River. A lot of times we would be going into a designated target which we struck every so often as authorized by the Department of Defense. We would see, out in the open, surface-to-air missiles being moved from one point to another. And, we couldn't strike. The North Vietnamese intelligence officials found out about our inability to take the initiative.

They thought, *Hmm...for some reason we are no longer being strafed. These guys fly right over obvious targets.*

So trucks and supplies totally traveled around whenever they wanted because we were not allowed to strike.

On the other hand, I think the Navy had a better agreement with the Department of Defense. They had asked for a preapproved set of targets.

They said, "We want to hold them in our hand and when we see the weather is right and they are vulnerable then we will strike them."

The DOD agreed. So sitting out in the Gulf of Tonkin the 6th Fleet could send a ship in and if they spotted a train on the tracks moving in their zone, they just had to designate the zone where the train is located and a set of targets inside that zone and then launch the fighters. They'd be there within minutes. Their response time was effective. But the Air Force was hamstrung. We couldn't do it.

I believe we could have crippled the North Vietnamese in the South, if we had been permitted to select our own targets and attack targets of opportunity. We could have stopped supplies right there in the North. As it was, we couldn't do it.

It was frustrating. One disgruntled pilot, as he was leaving the combat zone over Hai Phong harbor, rolled in and did some strafing on a Russian boat which was off-loading surface-to-air missiles.

It wasn't but just a matter of minutes after that attack was completed that it was known to authorities in the United States. An inquiry was set into motion for the purpose of finding who conducted the attack and who authorized it? Well, there was no authorization. I remember that I had happened to be out on a strike that day. To establish who did that shooting everybody who had fired their Gatling guns was called in before the wing commander.

He said, "You fired fifty rounds out of your gun. What did you shoot them at?"

I said, "Fifty rounds in a Gatling gun is a micro-second shot. That gun fires 6,000 rounds per minute. On the way into a combat zone we always fire a short burst to prove it's live. That was my proof shot after I got over enemy territory. "

He said, "Okay, go back to bed."

Finally he found somebody who had shot a thousand rounds or so. That was the guy who did the strafing run. It's a bad thing to be court martialed for strafing the enemy at one of their weak points when you discover it. That's a sad thing. It's a terrible way to fight a war.

Route Pack-6 – "Downtown"

I flew daily for the next nine days, repeating the *milk runs* to RP-1. The Wing policy was to send the newcomers on at least ten milk runs before going *downtown* to the Hanoi area. May 24, 1967, I joined a strike force of twenty Thuds on an attack on Phuc Yen Airfield, North Vietnam. I was the last fighter to roll in on the strike. The air was filled with puffs of smoke from the rapid firing 37mm and 57mm anti-aircraft guns. Rolling in on the target with a load of six 750 pound bombs, I was stunned at the sight I saw below through my reticule on the bomb sight. Hundreds of glowing, red projectiles rose from the target and seemed to be directed straight at my windscreen. In the last instant they all appeared to diverge and whistle by my craft.

The six seconds it takes to dive from 15,000 feet to the drop altitude of 7,500 feet is the pilot's *moment of truth*. The pilot must stabilize the craft's dive angle and airspeed before reaching the drop altitude to successfully hit the target. Those six seconds leave the pilot vulnerable to the anti-aircraft defenses. This moment of truth is much like the moment of truth a matador has as he goes over the horns of the bull to place the killing thrust of his blade between the bull's shoulder blades. The matador's soft under belly is exposed to the bull's horns in this moment. So it is with the pilots of the fighter bombers. The final six seconds of the pilot's attack gives the advantage to anti-aircraft gunner. It takes a great deal of concentration and fortitude to make a successful drop under these conditions.

All sixteen of us made it back to Takhli RTAB safely that day. We left Phuc Yen airfield thoroughly pocked up with twenty-foot craters that required a great deal of time and effort to repair. Since there was no point target but rather the entire airfield to hit, we all received congratulations by the intel-debriefers for our work that day. I was fatigued but jubilant with my first mission accomplished into *downtown* North Vietnam.

I flew virtually every other day from that day on. On the non-flying days, I had ground duties that included; serving as flight safety duty officer in the tower giving the tower control personnel advice as they managed the traffic, serving as mobile control officer at the takeoff end of the runway where I observed the configuration of the aircraft taking off, serving as Chairman of the awards and decorations committee for the squadron. And, as senior flight commander, I was tasked to schedule rest and recuperation (R & R) time for the combat crews. We tried to assure a three-day weekend to Bangkok for the crews every month.

Off Time/Recreation
During my tenure I was able to go R & R twice. We would catch the slow moving train from the village of Takhli to Bangkok. The trip was nearly three hours, stopping at every village to deliver and pick up mail and freight. At Bangkok we treated ourselves to a

stay at the Bangkok International Hotel. We languished around the pool and sipped Singha beer and forgot about the war for a while.

Piowaty, Griffin, Lawrence, and Lane from my F-105 checkout class were on the same duty schedule as I was at their squadrons at Takhli. We saw each other often at the O Club, the center of our social life on base. One day Piowaty approached me at the bar and said,

"Hey, Mo. Guess what I bought today."

"What?" I answered.

"A bicycle."

"Me too!" I said, astonished at the coincidence.

We not only wanted the exercise of biking the mile to work and back daily, but when we had a couple of hours of free time before dark we wanted to cruise through the countryside to meet some of the peasants and see their homes and work places. Piowaty and I shared the expense of buying one of the first models of Polaroid cameras. As we peddled through the countryside we met and photographed the people at the roadside kiosks and rest areas.

We gave the photos to the people, most of whom had never seen their image before. Piowaty photographed a young woman with a newborn baby snuggled to her breast. When he gave her the photo she broke into tears of joy. I photographed a young boy with a fledgling robin in his hands. When given the photo he shouted in astonishment, turned and raced across the rice paddies to show his mother.

Our wives sent us coloring books and crayons as well as whistles and yo-yos to take with us on our goodwill journeys. The children loved them! The bicycles allowed Piowaty and me to wind down from the tensions of combat occasionally by making a few people happy.

By mid-June I had twenty-five combat missions and perhaps a half dozen non-counters into Laos. I was seasoned enough to take a leadership role in the strike force. Lieutenant

Colonel Obadiah Dugan was the squadron CO at that time. Normally, one of the three squadron COs led the twenty ship strike force into RP-6. His Ops officer or senior flight commander flew deputy lead as number three in the first foursome of Thuds. If the Force Commander had to abort for some reason, the deputy continued the strike as lead. Dugan's new Ops Officer was Major Robert Donahue. Normally they flew together leading the Strike Force. Alternately, the new Wing Director of Operations Officer, Colonel Robert "Bob" White of X-15 fame, led the Force and I had the honor fly with him as his deputy.

Bob White, as a major, flew the X-15 into space by soaring to 59.6 miles which is beyond the upper reaches of the earth's atmosphere in 1962. He flew more than fifty missions during WWII before he was shot down over Germany in February of 1945 and taken prisoner. After the war he left the service to complete a degree in Electronic Engineering. He was recalled to service during the Korean War. Following that war he was assigned to Edwards AFB as a test pilot. Not only did he fly ten miles out of the atmosphere he was the first man to fly a winged aircraft at four, five and then six times the speed of sound.

Making a Very Big Hole

I think I found grace in the eyes of Colonel White on a non-counter mission in Laos June 18. The weather in the refueling zone was bad so the primary mission was aborted. White and I still had a generous amount fuel on board so he sent everyone in the Force back to Takhli except our foursome. He called the airborne command post, Red Crown, to report that he had a flight of four with heavy ordnance available for any alternate target they might have. Red Crown acknowledged and gave us a vector into Laos and the frequency to contact a Forward Aircraft Control (FAC) with a call sign of Covey 201. Arriving overhead of Covey 201 at 26,000 feet the FAC made contact.

"Glad to see you guys. You are just what I need. I have spotted a pin-wheel of 85mm anti-aircraft under construction," he said.

The 85mm is heavy artillery that can easily reach 26,000 feet. They are deployed in an array of six guns in a circle. The gunner sits in the middle of the circle with optical ranging sights and taps a foot trigger that fires each gun in turn, thus allowing the barrel a few moments to cool before firing again. The dive bomber viewing the sequential muzzle blasts from above sees a pin-wheel of deadly flashes.

"What's the target elevation, here?" White asked.

"1,500 feet. What's your ordnance?" Covey 201 asked.

"Two M118s each"

"What's a M118?"

"You'll see," White said.

The M118 is a 3000 pound bomb with an explosive content of 2000 pounds of Tritinal which creates a 125 foot wide crater and a kill radius of about a 6000 feet. White spotted the smoke Covey 201 had used to mark the target. He dipped his left wing sharply to call for an echelon-left formation. He set up the flight for a right hand roll in from 15,000 feet.

This looks good to me, I thought.

And it was, except we had two of the worse wingmen in the war zone. White insisted on using them. He was planning on the two of us doing the precision work anyhow. We rolled in a second apart into a 45 degree dive doing 550 knots. White, eager to place his bombs in the circle of 85mm gun barrels, pressed in below the proper drop altitude. The M118 has a very high kill envelope so the bomb has a seven second arming delay after release to keep the pilot from diving into the kill envelope of his own bombs. For this drop we should have released the bombs 7,000 feet above ground level or 8,500 feet. White's bombs smashed into the circle and buried themselves thirty feet into the ground without detonating.

White's wingman was notorious for dropping early to avoid getting too close to the anti-aircraft fire. His bombs detonated a mile short of the circle. I released my bombs at 8,600 feet just to be sure they had time to arm. I had adjusted the bomb sight for this altitude. The bombs detonated in the center of the pin-wheel sending six 85mm gun barrels spinning off into the jungle. Covey 201 shouted with joy,

"Sierra Hotel! What a blast. Great bombs, Three, great bombs. They will have to send out for more 85s now!"

My wingman started his pullout before he actually released his bombs. He tossed his bombs a mile beyond the circle, creating a 250 foot wide crater harmlessly in the jungle.

At the debriefing after the mission, White was complimentary of my bombing. He was a little embarrassed about duding his bombs by pressing too low for the kill. He was not concerned about our wingmen. I was furious with them but he shrugged it off. He said that not everybody is cut out for this work but they risked their lives trying. White used me for his deputy lead from then on when he led the strike.

MiG Hunting

One of the advantages of flying with Colonel White was that he had ambitions of shooting down a MiG during his tenure as Wing Director of Operations. After a strike in North Vietnam with him he would direct our wingmen to go home as a twosome so he and I could run up and down Thud Ridge MiG hunting. He wanted to shoot one down, or at least get a shot at one while he was in combat.

The Thud is not an agile air-to-air dog fighter but has great speed. Our tactic would be to overtake and surprise a flight of MiGs, strike, and then streak for home. As a twosome in spread formation we pushed the throttle up to 600 knots, which is really fast. We'd then buzz the ridges to spot a prey. It was difficult to get an anti-aircraft barrel to even track that fast as you flash by. You're not going to get shot down by anti-aircraft under those conditions.

We never really saw any MiGs. However, one time when we were doing this MiG search we spotted a flight of four unpainted aircraft. These appeared to be MiGs without camouflage painting on their aircraft.

Bob said, "We have a foursome dead ahead. I'm going to take the two on the left. You take the two on the right."

The two on the right would have been, as they were going away from me, aircraft three and four in the flight. And, as I was closing, I locked on to the number four guy. At that very moment he pulled out of formation and did a barrel-roll and pulled back into formation.

Bob White said, "Break lock! Break lock! It's the Navy!"

The Navy guys never could get serious about the war. Here's this Navy flyer; he's bored flying back to the carrier. So, he just pulls out and does a barrel-roll. His stunt saved us from making a bad mistake. Actually, we weren't going to fire until we made a positive ID anyway. We just left our afterburners going and streaked across the top of their formation, putting a sonic boom on them.

They heard "KA-BOOM" and a couple of Thuds go over their heads and streak out in front of them, disappearing in the stratosphere. They realized the Thuds were in town. But, we didn't shoot them. If the foursome had been the enemy, we could have each shot down a MIG. Probably the other two would have scattered.

North Vietnamese Defensive Weapons

Without a doubt, the North Vietnamese were not going to let us strike our targets with impunity. There were three basic weapons used by the enemy to deter our success. They had the air-to-air threat of Russian made MiGs flown by North Vietnamese pilots. There were the Russian made surface-to-air (SAM) missiles which locked on to the American aircraft by means of radar and heat sensing guidance systems. And, lastly, there were the hundreds of antiaircraft guns which were prolific in the target areas. And, I suppose there were the tens of thousands of small arms weapons and even rocks thrown by the ground troops and peasants. All in all, it was an effective arsenal that was a force to be seriously considered.

The enemy would shoot surface-to-air missiles at us at times. We would see them but they were poorly directed. The way you know that a surface-to-air missile has been shot and is not directed at you is you can see part of the white body of the missile itself. It looks like a white telephone pole streaking across the sky. The one which has your name on it looks like a cat's eye. And, when they fire them in pairs you see cat's eyes coming at you. You then need to take defensive maneuvers.

Their anti-aircraft facilities were ubiquitous; there were just so many of those. They were not located at the target sites, for they didn't want to be at the target and look up at F-105s coming down who could kill them. That's not a good shot anyway and gunner is likely to get killed in the battle. So, they put anti-aircraft in a defensive ring around a known target like the Bac Giang Bridge. That was the one I was shot down on. It had 138 guns around it according to our intelligence people. By the amount of shooting and flak bursting around me, I believe it.

But, it was an angular shot and a lot of parameters were changing for the gunner. As I was changing altitude and airspeed, the gunner had to make compensation for all of that. His projectile took six seconds to get up to me and I was only going to be in that chute for six seconds. So, he best have his act really together. He didn't have time to fire a shot, see where it traveled, make an adjustment, and then fire again. The day I got shot down some gunner made a good guess as I rolled in and fired two very accurate shots. I got two in the belly, while I was in a 45-degree dive going 550 knots.

Since we were jamming their radar fire control they used alternate tactics on us besides their optical manual tracking. They attempted to set their projectile fusing to create a wall of flak in an attempt to divert our intended flight. But that didn't work. We were changing altitude so fast their flak curtain was never in the right place to be intimidating. However, that didn't not stop them from trying. Dozens of anti-aircraft gun sites would fire in concert. It was astounding that there were so many guns, though, and so much flak. I can't describe it. None of the paintings I have seen about strikes can really accurately describe the target because there is so much flak smoke. There was a lot of shooting. It was their major defense.

Thai Nguyen Power Plant – "Downtown"

The summer of 1967 witnessed a devastating three or four months of battles that caused the loss of some fine men. On July 5th, I saw Major Ward Dodge take a direct hit from an 85mm anti-aircraft round. His plane exploded into flames. Two other men were lost that fateful day. Nevertheless, we continued to produce 1500 combat sorties per month from Takhli. Our sister Wing of Thuds, the 338th Tactical Fighter Wing operating out of Korat RTAB, produced the same number of sorties as well. The enemy defenses fought fiercely and effectively.

On a steamy hot day in early August, I flew as deputy Force Commander on a strike into North Vietnam to destroy the Thai Nguyen power plant, a vital facility producing seventeen percent of the nation's thermal electric power. Shortly after the inbound refueling, Lieutenant Colonel Dugan spotted a defect in his aircraft, requiring him to abort and return to base accompanied by his wingman. I took the leadership of the Force and proceed with the sixteen Thuds to the target despite marginal weather in the target area. The importance of destroying this target merited the risk.

We wound our way to the target area. There was a clear hole in the cloud deck. We would be able to see the target for the strike. Likewise, the anti-aircraft gunners could see us as well. I dipped my wing sharply to the left to set the Force in echelon-left. Nearing the power plant I pitched up to 15,000 feet and rolled in to the right. I placed my two M118s in the switching yard adjacent to the generator barn. Piowaty, flying two flights to the rear, placed two M118s through the barn roof into the generator room. The rest of the Force scattered the pieces left over.

Overhead the F-4s flying high cover to protect our force were engaging MIGs. One of the F-4s was damaged and one of the MiGs took a hit. Two of my Thuds in the force took minor anti-aircraft damage on the roll in. It was a fierce battle ably fought by both sides. However, our side left the power plant totally disabled.

The battle damaged aircraft made it home safely. The debriefing team examined the film from our aircraft and gave Piowaty and me credit for the target destruction. Later, the Awards and Decoration Committee nominated me for my first Silver Star for my role in the battle.

Having an opportunity to attack the Thai Nguyen Power Plant was certainly a relief from striking the same old targets over and over through the summer. Secretary of Defense McNamara and President Lyndon Johnson had a tight rein on which targets we were to hit and when we would hit them. They were amateurs at conducting a war and yet they were adamant about centralizing the targeting decisions. Many congressmen as well as the Joint Chiefs of Staff were pressuring them to allow Airpower to play a more effective role. Yielding a bit to the pressure a few more important targets were reluctantly released for targeting.

Doumer Bridge, Hanoi

Late in the evening of August 10th we were told that a really important target was being considered for the next day. I was excited to hear this. It was our squadron's time in the rotation to lead the Force and Colonel Bob White was going to be the Force commander. I had every chance to be a part of it. The target was held secret from the rank and file. But, the target identity was known to the staff at 7th AFHQ in Saigon. Several Colonels from the headquarters called Colonel White asking for a slot on the mission. White would have none of it. He wanted to hand pick the participants from the pilots he knew could put bombs on the target. He called me into his office to talk,

"Mo, Colonel Girardeau, the Wing Commander, wants me to use one of the Squadron Commanders for Deputy on this mission. I am going to lead the force with a foursome carrying CBUs. The first bomb flight will be Lieutenant Colonel McDonald as Bear flight. He will serve as Deputy Force Leader. Lieutenant Colonel Dugan will follow with Marlin flight. Lieutenant Colonel Norris has the third bomb flight and you will lead Scotch, the last bomb flight."

"Thanks Colonel," I said, "I wouldn't want to miss out on this one."

"I wouldn't want you to. I want you to nail this target if everybody else misses." He chuckled.

Early in the morning we met in the briefing room at Wing HQ. We learned that the target for the day was the Doumer Bridge at Hanoi. It was the longest bridge in North Vietnam. It was nineteen spans long and 58 feet wide. It was the major supply lane from China to Hanoi. Until now it had been sacrosanct because McNamara and LBJ prohibited us from striking the City of Hanoi or Gia Lam, the civilian airport just across the Red River. We were to attack the center span of the bridge in hopes of disrupting traffic flow into the City of Hanoi. I was thrilled to have the balcony seat of the attack by leading the last bomb flight to roll in.

This was a high visibility target. The presses around the world would be humming with the news of this escalation in the US efforts to interdict the flow of supplies to the war in the South. I knew that the North Vietnamese defenses would see that we were inbound to a vital area and would throw every defensive weapon they had at us.

After the morning briefing, the aircrews went to the O-Club for breakfast. Colonel White and I shared a table and a hardy breakfast of creamed beef on toast (SOS) and eggs.

"This is going to be fun!" I commented.

"And dangerous," he said.

"But that's the fun in it, isn't it?" I said.

"Yes, you are right, Mo. We are all adrenalin junkies," he commented soberly.

In order for the armament crews to configure the twenty aircraft to White's plan, there was a two hour delay in our normal departure and Time Over Target (TOT.) Finally, the twenty Thuds fired up and slowly made their way to the arming area at the end of the runway. As the arming crew removed safety pins from the ordnance, a Chaplain stopped by and made the sign of the cross to each of us before we departed for battle. It was comforting to see the Chaplain there blessing us in our hour of strife. Four by four we departed the base, joined up in formation and journeyed northward towards the inbound refueling area near Laos. The Force refueled to maximum capacity and proceeded northward to North Vietnam.

Red Crown began broadcasting bandit alerts meaning the MiGs were airborne and preparing to repel us. As we entered Route Pack-6, Iron hand, our Wild Weasel SAM suppressors began to alert us of the SAM sites coming up and preparing to launch SA-2 missiles at us. Captain Billy Sparks and his Electronic Weapons Officer (EWO) Major Carlo Lombardo flying the F-105F from our

357th FTS were among the four crews of Wild Weasels suppressing the SAMs for us. I felt comfortable to know that some of the best Wild Weasel crews in the Air Force had our back. This was going to be a red letter day in the annals of the war against the North Vietnam.

When the Force crossed the Red River into North Vietnam and reached Thud Ridge they turned right and shifted from their spread box formation into five foursomes in trail. The vector we flew was toward Hanoi and the enemy knew it. The SAM sights began launching SA-2 despite the Wild Weasels launching Shrike missiles at them.

The battle was on. I spotted two SAMs headed our way. However, they were misdirected and flying too high. I reported to Colonel White the SAMs going high over the Force; they were no threat. They were launched in a desperation panic by the missile men.

As the strike force drew nearer to Hanoi the SAM launches and the MiG warnings multiplied, but not one plane flinched. Five miles out, Colonel White raced out in front of the bomb flights. As a diversion he flew past the Doumer Bridge. Then he button-hooked back to sow CBUs on the AAA just as the bombers were ready to roll in. McDonald led Bear Flight in the roll-in that started the deadly strike.

At one second intervals his wingmen followed. In less than thirty seconds the entire Force had dropped their bombs and pulled out for regrouping and departure. From my balcony seat as last bomb flight commander I watched bomb after bomb after bomb sail across or slightly short of the 58 foot wide bridge span, sending great vertical plumes of water into the air.

Finally, the last man in Bear flight, Captain John Piowaty, placed one of his M118 3000 lbs bombs directly on the center span at the base of the supporting pylon. His smoke obscured the center span. I could not determine if the span had dropped or not.

Nevertheless, the rest of the bombers dropped their bombs where they saw the flash of Piowaty's bomb. Likewise, I dropped my bombs with the reticule over what I judged to be the place I saw Piowaty's bombs hit. My wingmen did the same.

As the Force exited the immediate target area, it became apparent that the anti-aircraft gunners had some limited success. Captain Bruce Lotzbier ran into a three-inch chard from an 85mm shell, shattering his wind screen and falling harmlessly onto the top of his instrument panel.

Bruce later reported, "The 500 knot airstream nailed me to my head rest. I was able to reach the seat adjustment to lower myself below its impact. For the remainder of the flight I stayed down in the fetal position, flying on instruments or looking out sideways. I was able to fly formation below my wingman to the emergency recovery base in Da Nang, South Vietnam, and set her down safely."

Bruce was not the only one hit. Through post-strike radio chatter I heard someone telling John Piowaty that he had fire burning in his speed brake area. I leaned on the throttle in hopes of catching John who must be just in front of my flight somewhere. I never caught him. John did not want to bail out over enemy territory so he lit the afterburner and streaked for friendly territory. On the way, his wingman told him the fire went out. John found that the hydraulic system supplying the speed brakes had caught on fire and depleted.

Unfortunately, that same system supplied the flaps and wheel brakes. John flew to Udorn. The brakes could be operated four times by use of an emergency air system for that purpose. John landed as slowly as possible. The plane dropped hard onto the runway because of the disrupted airflow across the tail. The drag chute popped out onto the runway intact, its main riser cut by the shrapnel of the 85mm slug that hit the tail. The right tire blew and the plane slewed toward the grass. With one application of the left brake on emergency air pressure, it was still slipping toward the grass. He dropped the hook, but the right outboard landing gear door caught the mid-field barrier and brought the plane to a halt.

John said, "Any landing you can walk away from is a good landing."

After our strike on the Doumer Bridge, a photo reconnaissance plane flew by for bomb damage assessment (BDA). The photos showed the center span of the Doumer Bridge missing. At the mission debriefing several guys were bragging that they hit the bridge. Actually they could not see their own bombs strike because they were in the pullout. Only the aft-looking camera or the guy behind you could verify where your bombs hit. The intelligence team reviewing the film never reported who actually dropped the center span.

I believe this was Colonel White's orders. Early when we flew the mission in Laos he regarded the scattering of the 85mm pin-wheel as a team effort where everybody risked their life. He felt the same about today's mission. He was not going to knight any one individual for the success of this mission. We all played a vital and risky role in what was accomplished that day.

The Wing Awards and Decorations Committee nominated Colonel White for the Air Force Cross and the bomb flight leaders for the Silver Star as well as the individual strike pilots for the Distinguished Flying Cross. I was honored to receive my second Silver Star within two weeks.

By this time Captain Richard Eugene had joined the squadron. Gene was formerly and Air Defenseman with experience in high altitude interceptors. Since we held a common background, we became friends immediately; a friendship that has lasted for over forty years. On that day I told Gene,

"I have to fly a mission just now but when I have time, I want to give you my *How not to Get Shot Down* lesson."

Combat activity heated up in August and I never had a chance to tell Gene my combat tips.

On the 23rd of August, 1967, Colonel White and I had breakfast together around three a.m.

I commented, "This has got to be the highlight of my quest for adventure. Nothing can top this!"

White, of X-15 fame, responded, "Don't say that. I've said that too many times only to be proven wrong the next day."

At that time I did not realize how prophetic his words would become.

The Shoot Down

On the day I was shot down Colonel White led the force striking the Bac Giang Bridge which was located eighteen kilometers northeast of Hanoi. I served as his deputy. White and his wingman spread cluster bomb units (CBUs) in an attempt to suppress the flack while I led the roll-in with fifteen other F-105Ds, each loaded with a pair of three-thousand pound bombs. Cluster bombs are particularly nasty little bombs the size of baseballs. When a canister of hundreds of these spherical bomblets is dropped from an aircraft, the unit separates into an array of bombs that makes many explosions covering a large expanse of area. They are not a precision destruction bomb. They are rather a means to suppress activity on the ground by damaging multiple targets. The objective is to keep the anti-aircraft gunners, on which they are being dropped, on their knees with their heads in the dirt.

It was *Clear and Visibility Unlimited* (CAVU) and all 138 enemy anti-aircraft gunners on the ground had a clear shot at the first man down the chute, which on this day would be me. There were 37mm and 57mm rapid firing anti-aircraft weapons with highly skilled gunners, each wanting revenge on us for damaging that same bridge thirty days earlier.

I dipped my wing left to signal all flights to change from their defensive formation to echelon-left formation. My wingmen now flew in a line off my left wing, waiting to follow my right-hand roll-in. I climbed from twelve thousand feet to fifteen thousand then rolled in rapidly to the right. Each fighter-bomber followed at one-second intervals. In less than twenty seconds the entire strike force would drop their load of bombs and streak for home.

Disaster struck!!

For sixty-one missions I had seen perhaps a million hot projectiles whiz by my aircraft in near-misses. I had learned to not let them distract me from the task of making an accurate drop. The odds caught up with me. I took two hits in the belly. Thunk-thunk! — it was like a sledge hammer had slammed the bottom of the fuselage. Neither the Thud nor I paid immediate attention to the hits. I was just a second away from reaching the drop point where air speed, dive angle and altitude were all correct for bomb release. I pickled (dropped the bombs) and then checked the damage. The *idiot panel* of emergency warning lights lit up like a Christmas tree. It gave out nonsense readings such as *Gear Down* and *Oxy Low*. I was already on fire. All of Vietnam could see the fire plume.

I attempted to pull out of the screaming dive but the control stick felt limp and impotent. The hydraulic pressure went to zero before I could get the nose up. I deployed the RAT, a small Ram Air Turbine used to provide emergency hydraulic pressure, to break the dive. When that emergency pressure was depleted, I electrically locked in the elevator slab and leaned back to take stock of the situation. My aircraft was now a high-powered, unguided missile that was streaking through the sky at 550 knots in a three-degree nose-low attitude. I had no control over the fate of the aircraft. This was not good.

I called "Shark three has been hit" which was not news to the thirteen thuds behind me who had just seen their leader torch.

The J-75 jet engine was still running in full afterburner. I was gaining speed, too much speed in fact.

The Flight manual of the F-105 states: "The maximum safe velocity for ejection is 550 knots....Ejection should not be delayed when the aircraft is descending and cannot be leveled out"

Since the dive bomb run usually exceeds this maximum I realized I needed to turn off the afterburner and throttle back to 550 knots or less. But the aircraft was nose low and wanted to gain speed. I had no hydraulic pressure to extend the speed brakes. Fortunately, each second was taking me further away from the enemy gunners and their intense barrage. Reluctantly, I eased the throttle back to slow to 500 knots.

I wanted to delay my exit as long as possible. But, there was great danger in delaying departure from a burning aircraft. The fire begins to eat its way forward, ultimately reaching the elevator slab. When this happens the slab falls away and the aircraft tumbles, destroying itself and the aircrew. I had to trust my wingmen to tell me what the deterioration progress was to avoid certain death. I had very few seconds that I could delay. I tightened the straps on my parachute and my oxygen mask to prepare for the wind blast that was to hit as soon as I ejected from the aircraft.

"I've got to punch out, see you guys after the war." I said, a moment before I ejected.

Jet fighters are equipped with powerful ejection seats that propel the occupant nearly 400 feet away from the aircraft. Although the ejection system is skillfully engineered, many things can go wrong, such as poor body position at the moment of firing, violent aircraft motion, speed that produces an impact air pressure that rips and tears clothing, and flailing arms and legs.

Practically all of these things happened to me. A split second before I squeezed the ejection seat trigger, the aircraft shuddered and lurched into a sharp pitch up and right turn, throwing my left foot out of the stirrup of the ejection seat. The seat fired at that very moment. A sharp blow to my extended left leg snapped my thigh. The dynamic force of the air steam ripped my helmet from my head and the gloves from my hands. I became a very highly trained rag doll hurling through the North Vietnamese airspace.

Three point five seconds after ejection, the seat automatically separated and the parachute automatically deployed. Suddenly, the din and excitement of the air battle stopped. I felt alone...very alone as I floated silently toward the earth.

The years of training jolted me into action. I reached for the hooked knife latched to my left leg in order to cut four parachute riser cords marked in red. This enabled air to spill from the back of the parachute canopy giving it stability and four to eight knots forward speed. The parachute then flies like a paraglider and can be maneuvered to a desirable landing spot. I noticed without interest that my thigh was broken, forming an odd knee at the break. The rest of the leg dangled below and swayed limply in the breeze. I felt nothing. The adrenalin rush of the bailout blocked the pain of the injury. That soon changed

After cutting the necessary cords, I withdrew an emergency hand radio from my combat vest and reported.

"This is Shark Three. I'm in the parachute. I can't make the high ground. No need to try sending a chopper."

The rescue helicopters known as Jolly Green Giants were standing by off shore and willing to try anything to recover a downed pilot. I was too far inland. A rescue attempt would be too dangerous. I did not want to be the cause of more losses. Besides, most successful pickups are from unpopulated ridges, I was over the rice fields and being observed by the populace on the ground as I descended.

Flying the last Thud to exit the strike zone, Colonel Bob White, bravely made a circle around my descending chute and offered me some advice in a low, quiet voice," Roger ... Make friends down there, Mo."

And then there was silence. The Thuds left. The guns stopped shooting. And the war became very personal as I slowly descended helplessly toward nineteen million bad guys. As one of my POW mates later commented, "I was no longer part of a twenty-man strike Force but rather a one-man assault force." In my case it was a one-man, one legged assault force armed only with a 38 caliber Smith-Weston Combat Masterpiece and a razor sharp meat cleaver strapped to my calf.

I thought, *this is going to be testy.*

Chapter 4
THE CAPTURE

I joined the Air Force with the ambition of finding great adventure while flying and fighting for my country. My part of the fighting had ended for now, but greater adventures were yet to come, adventures of a different kind. They were adventures of personal challenge where a warrior must stand nose-to-nose with the enemy, unarmed, every day in an endless struggle to maintain his personal integrity and the honor of his country. That struggle was continuous for me for nearly six years

The Villagers

When the strike force departed new sounds caught my attention. The sounds were angry, exited voices. My parachute canopy captured sound from four thousand feet below and focused it on me like a parabolic dish. The enemy had sighted me and was racing to the landing area to effect my capture. They didn't know I was too badly injured to attempt evasion. My combat survival training taught me, when badly injured, placing yourself in enemy hands offered the better chance of surviving to fight another day.

I steered the parachute towards a small group of grass huts flanked by a vast expanse of soft, muddy rice paddies. I splashed down near the huts, rolling into my good leg just before contact. Immediately, I sat up, positioned my broken leg in front of me, and released the billowing parachute canopy from my harness. I had arrived in enemy territory.

Rice grown in the rice paddies are a perfect product to grow in mountainous and wet environments. The paddies of Vietnam have a history that dates back to the Neolithic period. I had departed my familiar world and floated into a world foreign from any I had ever known. The native Vietnamese was a person who had lived a simple life centered on the agrarian culture of rice. The nearest comparison which comes to mind was the feudal system of the dark ages. The populace was easily swayed by political doctrine and had survived under the control and direction of various warlords and foreign armies for centuries. The basic life of the peasant was virtually indifferent to politics and focused on the cycle of planting and nurturing the rice crop. It was a pliable and fertile source for the socio-communist credo of Mao Tse Tung and Ho Chi Minh.

The young men of the villages had been indoctrinated for centuries to serve as warriors, fighting for causes they didn't fully understand. They were fiercely clannish and ferociously embraced whatever doctrine was fed to them. They were taught that the Yankee flying machines belched death and destruction and were evil. They were the reason their loved ones perished and their villages destroyed. So when presented up close and personal with the *air pirates* who flew them, they embraced that threat enthusiastically and violently.

A real live master of the death dealing air machine now lay in their rice paddy. As we were labeled by North Vietnamese propaganda, U.S. aviators were *black criminals* or *Yankee air-pirates*. Any intention of honorable treatment as a captured enemy combatant was a foreign concept to the villagers and it was beyond expectation for the captured airman to expect any. A dozen villagers splashed across the paddy towards me shouting unintelligible commands.

Slowly and calmly I raised my hands and said, "Okay, okay--don't get excited. I'm not going anywhere."

Men armed with machetes, an old rifle or two, and two-inch thick bamboo clubs seized me roughly and proceeded to strip every item of gear and clothing from me. One captor seized my handgun and stuck it to my temple, shouting threats in Vietnamese. Others snatched items and ran off with their trophies. I was left clad only in briefs.

Triumphantly, the oldest among them demanded I get up and hike out of the paddy at gunpoint. I indicated as best I could that I was injured. Unsatisfied with my response two men pounded me with their bamboo poles. I clasped my hand behind my knees to form a tight ball which protected my injury to some small degree during the beating. Eventually, my captors realized I was physically unable to walk. Frustrated, each man grabbed an arm, leg, or foot and roughly hauled me to the nearest empty grass hut.

As my captors half dragged, half lifted me from that field, I was certain I was near the end of my life. I offered a silent prayer of thanks to God for the thirty-five wonderful years I had experienced on this earth. I had a Tom Sawyer boyhood in Kennett, Missouri. I had a large, Christian family with plenty of brothers and a sister to teach me the rules of good behavior. I had a caring community which treated every child as their own. I had a beautiful wife, a daughter and a son. My thoughts were of gratitude. If I were to die this day, I felt I had received my fair share of earthly joy. The American fighting man takes the strength of his religion and national character into battle. Death did not frighten me as I entered the valley of the shadow of death. I mentally prepared myself for the villagers' wrath.

The small grass hut was choked with villagers, each intent on crowding forward to stomp, kick or strike the captured American *black criminal*. The teenagers soon discovered they could step on the swollen broken thigh, evoking a scream of pain. For what seemed forever the villagers took their revenge on the *Yankee air-pirate*.

71

Then suddenly the mistreatment stopped. An elderly villager dressed in a suit quietly coaxed the irate crowd to withdraw. A militia-woman medic remained with two old crones who hovered over me to mumble advice to any who would listen. The medic glared at me as she prepared a hypodermic of clear liquid. I attempted a smile of thanks for the first kind act by the captor thus far. Without any reciprocal show of compassion, she injected my swollen thigh and darkness swept over me.

Several hours later I awoke to find the old crones were probing my mouth with dirty, withered fingers, admiring my two molar gold crowns. Half dazed, I wondered if they were planning to extract the gold crowns for their trophy. I did not realize at the time, but they had washed the mud and blood off of me. The militia woman approached and fed me a cup of sweet canned milk perhaps treating me for shock. Once again she injected my thigh and I lost consciousness while wondering if I would lose my gold crowns to the old crones before I awoke.

Later I awoke to find the crones still hovering over me. I quickly ran my tongue over the crowns to assure they were still in place, relieved that they were. This time, however, the old crones were admiring the cut of my briefs. They gestured and marveled at the cleverness of the fly. As the medic once again injected my thigh I thanked God for preserving my gold crowns and asked him to save my *Fruit-o-the-Looms* too.

The third awakening was to the rough hands of men placing me on a large wooden slab which served as a litter. Actually, it was part of a bed that the peasants put atop two wooden sawhorses. I was carried from the grass hut into the darkness. I was crammed violently into the back of a small truck to be transported to four other villages where the captured aviator was to be displayed. At each stop the villagers were permitted, and even encouraged, to pound on the prisoner to show their hatred of the *American*

Imperialist. Any sort of humiliation short of maiming or killing the captured airman seemed to be fair game.

Later discussions with other POWS revealed a variety of receptions by the villagers. Captain Irby David Terrell , B-66 navigator captured that summer, related his village ordeal to me. He said the leader of the village allowed each villager to deal him one blow. He was tied to a straight-backed chair and the villagers lined up. Dave observed that the first in line was a small, older lady. He doubted she could hurt him very much. To his surprise, the little old lady rushed forward and punched him so hard in the mouth that the chair fell over backward. The rest of the villager blows were just a blur to him after that.

Captain Robert Craner and Guy Gruters, a crew flying the two-placed F-100, were shot down near the DMZ the same summer. They were stripped of their clothes and boots and held in a grass hut several hours until the photographers arrived to make a news reel. They were given their flight suits and boots and taken out into a large field. Then they were marched back in the direction of the cameras by a fourteen year old girl carrying an ancient bolt-action rifle. The villagers watched from a distance. The captured airmen were made to kneel before the cameras.

At that moment, Gruters said, "A little old lady winged in a sweet potato from the crowd of villagers like Mickey Mantle throwing for home plate. The potato hit in the back of my head and knocked me flat on my face. My eyes were crossed by the blow."

Another story was tapped through the walls of Hoa Lo Prison by a prisoner who reported he was shot down in late December and stripped of his clothes and boots and made to march deep into the night time.

He reported, "Then we came to a levee and stopped. It looked like a perfect spot for them to stand me up for a firing squad. An officer came over and offered me a cigarette. I said, 'No thanks, I'm trying to quit'. An NCO with an AK-47 shouted at me and fired a few rounds into the levee. I said, 'Okay, okay, gimme a smoke.' We all lit up and puffed through a couple of cigarettes on our midnight-marching break.

"I thought to myself, *Ah, here I am in my underwear in a December night, having a couple of smokes with my new-found buddies. You just can't buy memories like that.*"

Finally, after visiting the neighboring villages, the small truck arrived at a clearing where a huge Russian helicopter awaited to fly me to Hanoi under the cloak of darkness. The villagers had finished with me and I had survived. I had entered into a nightmare where each successive encounter had only one desired outcome — survival. However, at that moment I didn't know within the hour I would have an even closer brush with death — another test of survival.

The Mob

The helicopter transporting me from the villages to Hanoi was huge. It was of Russian make capable of lifting heavy loads. A leather thong secured my elbows behind my back binding me tightly. Lying on my back, only my buttocks and elbows touched the metal floor of the helicopter. The twenty-minute ride to Gia Lam Airport in Hanoi jolted and jostled me until the hide was worn from my elbows. This minor abrasion was to be the least of my worries for this night.

At Gia Lam Airport the helicopter landed in the midst a large crowd which was assembled for the occasion of my arrival. The crowd was enlivened and restless. Approximately two thousand strong, they seemed to want blood. A speaker addressed them with a bullhorn. His impassioned speech seemed to crescendo and the crowd noise rose. Each declaration seemed to infuriate the crowd more. At the climax of the inciting speech a hundred hands reached into the helicopter and dragged my body into the crowd.

They pounded, punched, and kicked me. As I was passed through the crowd, each man who carried me twisted and jerked the limb he held. The man holding my injured left leg found that, because the thigh bone was completely broken in two, he could twist my foot 180 degrees to where the toes pointed exactly opposite of the right foot. Moreover, when he did this I was compelled to scream to the top of my voice. The mob cheered to hear me express the pain. So the man continued to twist, I screamed, and the mob cheered over and over again. It was a sadistic and excruciating game.

The man holding my healthy right leg seemed disappointed to discover he could not evoke the same loud screams from me regardless of how he twisted and bent that leg. Furiously, he dug great gouges of soft skin from the back of my right knee with his finger nails to show his hatred of the American prisoner.

The mob had been incited and was unpredictable and violent. If the carriers had dropped me to the tarmac, I feel sure the mob would have stomped me to death. I fought to remain at waist level and by so doing accept whatever punishment that might bring.

After perhaps three hundred yards of torture at the hands of the mob, we arrived at the door of a jeep. Someone of great authority demanded the mob thrust me into the back seat. Military guards piled in with me. Then the jeep sped away from the angry horde.

Somehow I felt more secure in the hands of the military. True, they were professionals at torturing prisoners but they knew their art better than the mob. Their intent would be to apply great pain in order to gain information but not kill.

There are accounts where downed flyers were reported captured but vanished — only to become footnotes in militia field reports. Such was the case of Lieutenant James Patterson and Lieutenant Commander Eugene McDaniel. Uninjured in the shoot-

75

down McDaniel survived captivity and was eventually returned in 1973. However, Patterson was reported to have a badly broken leg at the time of capture.

Three months previously, on May 19, 1967, the two flyers comprised the crew of an A-6A, one in a flight of six aircraft on a combat mission against the Van Dien repair facility located five miles south of Hanoi. During the course of the operation a missile was launched and detonated near their aircraft damaging it. The two airmen ejected from the crippled bird and two good parachutes were reported. As was typical, there was a successful attempt to contact both flyers once they reached the ground. In fact, ground communication continued until May 22nd. The two flyers were separated from each other but safely on the ground. McDaniel reported no injuries; however, Patterson indicated that he had a severely fractured leg.

The two flyers lost touch with each other. McDaniel believed his friend had been captured as he had been. He was even informed, at a later date, by an interrogator that Patterson had been capture, had a broken leg, but was all right. Although Patterson's name was heard in the prison communications system he was never confirmed by the returning POWs to be alive in the prison system.

In December of 1990 a U.S. field team investigating the whereabouts of unaccounted flyers located documents and interviewed Vietnamese witnesses associated with this case. The witnesses confirmed one pilot had been captured, but was also informed the second airman had been shot to death by militia on the fourth day after the shoot-down. With a severely broken leg and in a weakened state it appears Lieutenant Patterson was not worth the effort to care for. Apparently, he had lost his worth.

The military interrogators realized a prisoner was valuable to them in three ways: initially to acquire pertinent military information, then to dispense propaganda, and finally as a trading pawn for future political concessions. As long as the captured pilot had value to them, the flyer would be permitted to survive. The mob acknowledged none of this; their purpose was revenge which included maiming and killing if possible. The mob scene was my closest brush with death so far.

An hour later the jeep rumbled into a dark street and turned into a narrow passage with tall metal doors. I had arrived at Hoa Lo Prison, the dreaded Hanoi Hilton. Built by the French Colonialists a hundred years ago for imprisoning Vietnamese, the walls of stone stank with filth, vermin, and misery. The horror of this night was not yet over.

POW Code of Conduct

The Code of Conduct as it originally was written was really emphatic as to what the captured airman should do as an American fighting man. We could not accept parole. We provided only name, rank, and serial number and date of birth. And, that was not tenable. We knew it wouldn't be. As we were going through our Southeast Asia survival school training they told us, "This isn't going to work. You're going to get beat up badly if you stick to this. What you do is say as little as you can and use evasive techniques." They counseled that if we ever did get pressured into doing something like the writing the names of people who were in our squadron, simply fabricate a list.

An example was where a prisoner was writing the names of people and he wrote: Dick Tracy, Captain Marvel and so on. The story goes that the North Vietnamese were so proud of that list they went to the Paris Peace Accords with it. During the course of the Paris Peace Talks they produced the list and proclaimed, "Even the prisoners are helping us to win the war by giving us this information." And they read that list.

The American side laughed at them and said, "Thank you for that." They didn't at that time expose the farce for they were wary of retribution on the prisoner who provided it. Nevertheless, the North Vietnamese delegates were bragging about how they had cowed the men.

Eventually the reality of the farce filtered back to the higher ups in the communist echelon. A directive was issued saying, "Stop that! Never take anything they write down to the Paris Peace Talks. You let us read it first."

There were somewhere in the neighborhood of two-percent of the captives who didn't intend to put up a resistance which would cause them any discomfort—who collaborated with the enemy. There were twelve of those out of 600. That is two-percent.

These men were isolated from us because the rest of us were saying, "Hey! Don't do that. Don't edit their copy for Hanoi Hannah, taking out the awkward Asian phrases and putting in the idiomatic English. Obviously, it helps the Gooks." So they isolated those guys from the rest of the American prisoners.

We also heard later on that the collaborators actually had a different confinement than we did. In the propaganda photos you can see them as a group grinning and laughing. Also, you can see well cut pajamas much thicker and well-made than the stripes we wore. You can always identify the collaborators by their well-groomed pajamas with buttons.

Their treatment consisted of being locked up at night. However, they had a courtyard to walk around in during the day. The North Vietnamese just opened the cell doors and let them all out. I understand they even had an occasional beer for special occasions that the North Vietnamese were observing.

Years later when we all were repatriated, we tried to court-martial those who had made no attempt to resist exploitation by the captors—who rather had assisted the enemy in their propaganda programs. The Department of Defense was discouraged by Richard Nixon, however, who said, "This is a time for healing not a time for bashing people. If you don't feel these people have performed their service very well then ease them out of the service — silently." The general public was unaware that these men were removed from service with something other than an honorable discharge.

There was also a rumor circulating through the walls of the prison community, indicating there were some guys who did not received very harsh treatment at their initial interrogation; and, therefore, they must have compromised the Code. That was a nasty rumor and totally wrong.

Most of the body of the POW core realized that everybody had their own threshold of pain. Self-pride took a man up to that threshold. Beyond that a man was going to lose it. He had to yield something and make some kind of effort to get out from in under more pain than he could endure. And that may be a whole lot lower for some men than other guys.

It simply was not acceptable for others to criticize anybody about their resistance level. Unfortunately, some just didn't have the ability for extreme resistance in them. I know a lot of guys who took only two hours in the quiz room and upon returning said "I can't do that again. I can't get down on my knees anymore." I have no problem with that.

Interrogation Policy of the North Vietnamese

Thus began my initial interrogation stage of captivity. These first days were critical to the North Vietnamese. For within these few days the prisoner was at his most vulnerable state. He was disoriented and confused, definitely frightened, and most likely injured. And, most importantly he was alone, separated from family and friends and cut off from any assistance or support of his buddies and fellow warriors. He was in a very new and different world surrounded by people physically different from him who spoke a strange language and communicated with rage and often spat on him and inflicted terrible physical punishment, to say the least.

The North Vietnamese possessed no skill in interrogation which used guile and finesse, as was used in World War II by the Germans.   Our captor's sole approach was to demand unquestioned cooperation. If and when we did not comply, they went straight to the far end of the spectrum and applied heavy pain--torture. And, that torture was intense. It was something you simply could not resist. It was overwhelmingly painful.

The early shoot-downs reported to me that in 1965 and after, for a few months when the North Vietnamese first began to collect prisoners, they did not know what to do with them. Ho Chi Minh soon straighten them out by instructing his men to treat the American flyers as *black criminals*.   If the prisoners refused to cooperate and answer the questions put to them by the interrogators, they were obliged to feel free to beat them as they saw fit, because the captured airmen were of the same category of rapists and murderers.   In the eyes of Ho Chi Minh and his followers, the prisoners deserved neither creature comfort nor any human rights.

Therefore, when the North Vietnamese captured a prisoner and demanded, "What's the next target Hanoi?" his fate was sealed. For, the poor pilot was unable to provide that information because there was no discussion with the pilot in his mission briefings as to where he was likely to be going the next day. So as a result, the interrogators went straightway to heavy duty torture as a standard operating procedure. Obviously, they had direct orders from higher authorities to do so.

Intimidation in the form of heavy torture was routine under the Ho Chi Minh regime. We had been made aware of that through our training and we knew how to try to avoid going to a nose-to-nose confrontation. We were to attempt to evade their questions and feign, "I can't understand your English," "I'm too badly injured and I need help," or "I haven't had any water in two days" — whatever we could do to divert their attention from moving to absolute, head-on, heavy duty torture. However, almost every able bodied man ended up being tortured in some way. This was the Ho Chi Minh policy early on.

There had been prisoners captured from 1965, a full two years before I arrived in the prison camp on August 23rd, 1967. The interrogators were accustomed to using torture by the time I got there. The POWs mostly just danced the fine line. With brinksmanship you tried your best to avoid conflict and evade answering whenever possible. In the end they obtained very little useful information in their harsh initial interrogations.

The interrogators broke some people up so badly they got them to make propaganda for the enemy. They made them record taped messages for Hanoi Hannah, for instance. The broken prisoner proclaimed, "I'm here and getting good treatment," and some other lies. Sometimes the contrite prisoner even encouraged the fighting man down south to not "oppose these people they have a legal and just cause." That was the kind of propaganda they were looking for. History will surely record the treatment was harsh on the American POW, and it was brutal and bone breaking. I suspect we lost a lot of people in the initial interrogation just through the overwhelming pain of it.

The most brutal of the methods was the ropes. This horribly painful torture technique was applied to many of the American prisoners on their first encounter with the captor. They described it in detail in their repatriation debriefings. The torturer bond the wrists and elbows so tightly that the shoulder sockets were pulled out of place and the pectorals were stretched beyond belief. The ankles and knees were bound as well. With the prisoner seated flat on the floor. The torturer lifted the bound arms, forcing the body into a tight "C" shape. At this point the prisoner was literally looking at his own scrotum. A small rope was then tied from the wrists to the ankles. The prisoner was left in this horrible position for hours.

Our captors also employed other methods of torture such as beating your bare bottom with a truck fan belt. This cut the flesh right off of the prisoner. That was horrible. And in my case, if the prisoner had a broken limb like my femur, they kicked on that and got your attention right away. John McCain, for instance, had both his arms broken. With wounds similar to his the North Vietnamese twisted the injured limbs like a crank on a Model-A in order to force him to pay attention and get serious about his responses.

There were very, very few people who did not get initial interrogation torture. Those were odd cases though—exceptions to the rule. There was Captain Thomas Moe, an Air Force pilot of an F-4 fighter who was shot down by his own bomb on January 16, 1968. A faulty fuse detonated a bomb he was carrying. His aircraft commander in the front seat was rescued but Captain Moe was captured. During his initial interrogation Tom got knocked off the stool by a blow from a guard right away to get his attention. The blow and/or the fall knocked him out. He went into a comma for a full week. By the time he awakened from the comma, other prisoners had been captured and had preempted Tom. Because of his week-long comma, he missed his initial interrogation. The rest of us were envious of his technique.

Nevertheless, we experienced absolute torture during that period. Understand, this was the treatment throughout the downtown Hoa Lo main prison, the Zoo, which was an equally big prison south of town, the Zoo annex, and all of the satellites such as the Briarpatch, Camp Hope, and others which held prisoners. The treatment of prisoners and the disregard for their human rights, their creature comforts, and their medical problems were almost uniform throughout all the camps. And, it stayed that way until Ho Chi Minh passed away in September of 1969.

After the passing of Ho Chi Minh we saw almost immediately an improvement in the treatment of the American POWs. In addition, people at home began to get indications from all sorts of intelligence that the prisoners were being treated badly, particularly in initial interrogation. The public back home saw propaganda films where individuals were being made to bow in front of the enemy and they knew that was just a humiliating thing to military guys. So the pressure was on the North Vietnamese to change their way of treating prisoners. Actually, I think the North Vietnamese concluded it was counter-productive anyway. More often than not, when the North Vietnamese had beaten a prisoner into submission, the information they received from it was usually nonsense.

They wanted us to confess our sins and ask Ho Chi Minh for forgiveness, and provide some kind of false confession; we never did that. It seems like the enemy would be satisfied with a *sorry statement* like, "I came to bomb bridges and railroad tracks and not people. If anybody got hurt, I'm sorry." That seemed to be able to fill their square for having a piece of paper in our folder saying we were contrite.

We all seemed to have had some crisis along the way where the North Vietnamese wanted to get that piece of paper and put it in the folder. Once they obtained that scrap of paper with the *sorry statement*, they didn't pursue written statements thereafter.

The Rat noticed my file contained no false confession in January of 1969 before Ho Chi Minh died. They were capable of using terrible punishment. But, at that time they didn't have the manpower to assign a couple of heavy duty thugs to put on me to beat me up badly. So, they placed me in a cold cell. That's a cell which is open to the elements and where only bars were located in all the openings.

In the middle of January daytime temperatures were near 55-degrees F. They removed my blankets and every source of warmth, leaving me in my thin prison house pajamas. I shivered myself into hypothermic exhaustion in about five hours. In addition, the North Vietnamese attempted to keep me awake all day and night by having the guard kick the door on his rounds and get me up. However, the night guard was less efficient. He had to make his rounds every hour, which took him about twenty minutes to accomplish.

So, I received a fifteen minute nap every hour out of those nights. I didn't go into hallucinations as sometimes you'll do when you are guarded constantly where they can keep you awake. After ten nights, my North Vietnamese captors were satisfied with a *sorry statement* and I was returned to my cell. Carrigan, my cell mate said he was worried about me because they left my blankets and gear there in the cell. He thought I might not ever be back. He was apologetic about using my blanket during my cold soaking.

As indicated earlier, the harsh treatment suddenly changed when Ho Chi Minh died. We recognized it when the North Vietnamese came and removed the bricks they had covering the barred windows. Most of the windows we had in these prison camps had steel bars and louvered windows on the outside. But Ho Chi Minh wanted to have us confined and denied visual contact with anybody. So, he had them brick up those windows. And, the week he died they came around and took down the brick.

We were allowed to see outside and we could actually see other prisoners being moved back and forth. We couldn't actually talk to them; but, we could see them. Communications between rooms picked up because we could *flag* out the windows as well as tap on the walls, which was our normal method of communication.

We also recognized the fact that when we were summoned into a quiz, given some kind of propaganda lecture, asked to make propaganda ourselves, and then refused there was no punishment. We didn't get beat up. There was a new spirit of *live and let live* from that point on. We suspected, if we did not show disrespect to the guards or touch them, we could possibly continue our confinement without further beatings, as was generally the case from September of 1969 on.

I didn't receive any harsh treatment after that. They often wanted you to write down what you had been taught that day and we wouldn't do that. I always refused after the interrogations to write anything about what they had said. I later discovered, through conversations with other POWs, treatment had changed from *black criminals* status to *live and let live* status in the outlying camps also.

The Blue Room in New Guy Village

My personal initial interrogation began immediately upon arriving at Hoa Lo late at night soon after my capture. This was in August of 1967 while the interrogators were still following the brutal torture tactics of Ho Chi Minh. The litter bearers dumped me unceremoniously on the floor of the initial-interrogation room known to the prisoners as *The Blue Room*. This was a special room located in *New Guy Village* of the Hanoi Hilton. This was not a permanent home, but rather a way-station during the period of initial interrogation. I would spend my next twenty days here as a special guest of the North Vietnamese communists. Painted sky blue the walls were covered with rough gobs of plaster to dampen the screams of the tortured captives.

A table with a spot light lamp sat in the middle. From a straight-backed chair the interrogator demanded information from the prisoner who usually sat on a short three-legged stool. Two or three guards attended the session to apply physical punishment to the prisoner for non-responsiveness, impoliteness, or any other reason the interrogator chose. I lay on the bamboo litter and stared up at the yellow glare of the spotlight.

A greasy-faced North Vietnamese with a shock of black, unkempt hair and droopy eye leaned over me--the interrogator, known as *The Bug*. Colonel Robinson Risner, who was the Senior Ranking Officer of the American POWs at that time described the sadistic, ruthless man in his memoirs <u>The Passing of The Night</u>, Random House, 1974.

He wrote, "The Bug was about five foot three inches, with a round face. (By the time we left he was so fat he looked like a small Buddha.) His right eye had more white than the left, and was also kind of cocked. When he became excited, it would veer off at an angle. Sometimes it looked like a false eye. He would always emphasize everything by holding his finger at about a 45-degree angle above and in front of his head. He would get angry and start shouting. The bad eye would look off at a tangent, and, look out, beware! Something bad was coming."

The Bug spoke the first English words I heard in North Vietnam.

"So! The fat is in the fire," he said.

I thought, *it's ludicrous that after the ordeal I've experienced I have to face an interrogator who wants to practice using his English idioms.*

I struggled to think of a snappy response.

I could only retort, "And a stitch in time saves nine!"

"Exactly," said Bug.

We were speaking the same English language. Nevertheless, much was often lost in translation. To them the words were to be taken literally with no understanding of slang or regional American vernacular. The North Vietnamese interrogators generally were not well educated, at least by the same standard as the men they were interrogating. As such the prisoners often used their misunderstanding of the language against the interrogators to their own benefit. Feigned confusion regarding terms and words used by the interrogators worked well and often bought precious time for the prisoner.

The language divide was illustrated in an interrogation encounter of First Lieutenant Richard Bates, whose F-4E Phantom was shot down in October of 1972. The account is recorded in the

Minneapolis-St. Paul Star Tribune, November, 10, 2003. One of his interrogators threatened him time and again in broken English, saying, "You must cooperate or you will be Spanish!"

This time the confusion was honest. Truly confused, Bates delayed addressing the topic as he attempted to understand what was being said to him. Soon he realized, however, the threat was meant to say he would be *punished*. In an interview, Bates stated he almost laughed at the error when it happened, but restrained; he was fortunate that he did.

Although unaware that his response to me was totally incongruous with the context, Bug was satisfied that I understood my situation and there was no error in translation or communication. He began his work, which was to discover the next target to be bombed. My job was to evade answering the question for at least twenty-four hours or possibly until the next air strike, at which time the question was no longer important. Lying there in the floor clad only in briefs, choking mad with thirst, and with a throbbing broken leg I realized it was going to be a long, long twenty-four hours.

The Initial Interrogation

"What new target in Hanoi?" demanded The Bug.

He was one of the most sadistic interrogators of Vietnam. He glared at me with one wide eye that was filled with malice and hatred for the American intruder. Choking back the panic and terror of the circumstances, I struggled to remember the techniques of interrogation resistance taught to me in combat survival school at Fairchild AFB prior to joining the war effort. We were trained to show confusion; feign lack of ability to concentrate, request medical attention, food and water but avoid direct refusal to respond. We tried to control the situation in order to avoid severe torture that might lead to us revealing everything. We tried to hold out until the next air strike or at least for twenty-four hours.

The Bug set about his work and I set about mine. He demanded direct answers and I evaded revealing anything important in a thrust-and-parry struggle which lasted for hours. The game was deadly and called for brinkmanship on the part of the prisoner. When the Bug lost patience with my poor responses, he called the waiting guards. At The Bug's command they deftly twisted my left foot to inflict maximum pain to the injured thigh. My screams fell on deaf ears and stoic faces. They had done this many times before and lost their sympathy for human suffering.

Dawn came and reminded The Bug of his weariness. As the session ended I took pride in myself for telling them nothing they could not have learned by standing on the street corner and watching the air strike. Namely, that I was an F-105D strike pilot. We struck the Bac Giang Bridge. There were twenty of us. And, we avoided dropping on populated areas. So far so good--the evasive techniques were working.

Suddenly, the Bug jumped to his feet and screamed in mock anger. "Your answers are not satisfying! You do not cooperate. You only want to talk about your injury. You cannot blame us for that. You did it to yourself. I hope it rots. Then we throw you away with it. We do not fix. You do not deserve the humane and lenient treatment from the Vietnamese people. I go now to ask the high authorities to have you shot."

His sudden tirade was not in keeping with his weary mood during the last hour. The Bug stomped out, unaware that I recognized the *Good-Guy-Bad-Guy* interrogation technique. I calmly waited for the *Good Guy* to replace The Bug.

As I lay in the bamboo liter catching my breath I noticed dawn had arrived. People noises could be heard as the day began, I noticed an air vent high on the wall. It was about four by eight inches in size. Through it I could see blue sky and a single twig of a tree branch. Then briefly a sparrow landed on that twig, looked in my direction and peeped a single note. Then cheerfully flew away. I was cheered by that moment. I was reminded of the old hymn lyric that says "If His eye is on the sparrow, you know He's watching you."

I realized that I should not let these Godless interrogators terrorize me. God is still in charge of my fate. Even if I die in this dismal room, I should not worry. It will be part of God's plan for me. I relaxed. I smiled. I realized that this ordeal is part of a larger, more important plan that is being played out. From that moment on I wore that faith like armor. I was not afraid to die. The North Vietnamese could not understand it. But, Americans are not fearful of death and are hard to terrify into cooperation with their will.

Within minutes a pencil-necked, well-groomed Vietnamese Lieutenant arrived. He was dubbed *Soft Soap Fairy* or *Happy Dan* by the prisoners. He bent over my litter pretending to be shocked at my obviously poor physical condition.

"Are you in pain?" he asked. "Would you like some water?"

I was choking for water and he knew it. I accepted a cup of smelly, warm water. His low-volume, soft voice was to deceive the prisoner into believing that a kind, sympathetic interrogator had arrived. We practiced dealing with this teamwork interrogation in survival school. Happy Dan's role was to gain my confidence and cooperation with a soft approach. He began as predicted.

He said, "Do you know you made that other interrogator very angry? He is a very powerful man in this camp. He has gone to ask permission to have you eliminated. I do not want that to happen to you. You must tell me what is the next target to be bombed in Vietnam so that I can intervene on your behalf."

His English was impeccable.

"Forget it," I said, "I'd be better off dead anyhow." I gambled. I did not want to get caught in their *good-guy/bad-guy* loop. Actually, I was not lying. At this point, living was more difficult than dying. However, I was not willing to give up yet

"But, what about your children? They depend on you. They need a father. And, what about your lovely wife? She needs you." He said.

"Nah, she's already looking for my replacement," I answered.

Happy Dan attempted to conceal his look of disgust. Orientals mate for life and believe Americans trade our mates as often as automobiles. I let him continue to believe it. I denied him an emotional lever on me.

The *good-guy* is at a disadvantage in this game. He must play a non-violent role. I counted on that. I needed the respite to regain my strength. I knew the *bad guy* would return. I kept Happy Dan on the string as long as I could. The breather only lasted a couple of hours.

The Bug returned with his sleeves rolled up. He was losing the battle and he sensed it. He brought a heavy-fisted muscle man with him that the prisoners called *Nook*. Nook loved the feel of his fists smacking into human flesh. He grinned as he worked.

The Bug demanded answers. I evaded. Nook pounded. The time wore on. I became unconscious more than once during Nook's punching. I lost track of time. Was it day or night? Has it been twenty-four hours yet?

Near the end of my strength, I responded to The Bug "I don't know the next target to be bombed. Since you don't believe me I will have to start lying!"

"No!" said The Bug. "You must not lie."

"Then I will have to guess," I said with false resignation.

"Okay, I allow you to guess." he conceded.

He held a map of Hanoi over my litter. Through the blood and sweat I strained to see a believable, but unlikely, place.

"There, maybe there" I said, pointing to a spot on the map.

The Bug looked at my selection. His jaw tightened.

He snorted "That shows you do not cooperate. That is the Thermal Power Plant. It is already destroyed!"

Furious, he started to beckon Nook to administer more punishment. Suddenly the wail of air raid sirens changed his anger to fear. Quickly he gathered his maps in order to race to a shelter.

"I am not through with you. You will give me more of your knowledge in the future. I must go now. There will be other *air pirates* shot down that I must interrogate. I will be busy but we will meet again!" He said hastily as he and Nook exited the interrogation room.

The first day of my initial interrogation phase had ended. I took a deep breath. With battered lips I smiled from ear to ear, lying there alone in the middle of the torture room, listening to the music of roaring jet engines from a couple of dozen F-105 Thuds and the rhythm of the huge three-thousand-pounders destroying a nearby bridge.

The Second Day

The following day, 24 August 1967, was interesting but not violent. The Bug had apparently turned my interrogation over to some subordinates. I sensed that he did not want the poor results so far accredited to his efforts. Early in the day a guard entered the Blue Room with a piping hot tin cup full of tea. I was choking mad with thirst but could only sip the tea slowly without scalding myself.   An hour later an unknown interrogator came in and launched into a speech about how my fate hinged on my cooperation with him. I listened without emotion and waited for his demands. Finishing his preparatory motivation talk he revealed his subject. He said:

"Now, you must tell me what a 'mil' is." He pronounced the word like meal.

Confused, I only stared back at him quizzically.

Again and again he repeated his question. I could see he was getting on the edge of resorting to the application of significant pain. I honestly did not understand what he wanted and was not going to start guessing. I did not think *"Two over easy and a side order of bacon"* was a prudent answer. Further, it probably would only get me the broken leg stomping act again.

Finally, he stomped out of the room in a huff. I steeled myself for the muscle men that were undoubtedly going to show up. Surprisingly only the interrogator reappeared. He held in his hand a 5x7 index card with columns of numbers that represented settings for our gun sight and bombing reticule. (Artillerymen found it more convenient to divide the compass into 1000 *mils* rather than 360 degrees.) Such cards are sometimes clipped onto a pilot's kneeboard as a reference to preparing for his dive bomb run. Upon ejection, kneeboards and maps are scattered to the four winds. They are not secret by any means. Our survival training taught us not to get into conflict with the enemy trying to preserve information that could be found in a dictionary.

Wearily I shrugged and said, "It's like an inch."

He said, "Ah hah!" and left the room, not to be seen the rest of the day.

Around 10:00 a.m. I was offered a bowl of watery green soup and a chunk of bread about the size of a dinner roll. Two guards lifted my liter and carried me to an area known to the prisoners as *New Guy Village.* It was a row of cells close to the Blue Room used to hold prisoners being regularly interrogated. I was unmolested until the following day.

The Third Day

I was carried to the Blue Room after a morning meal of soup and bread to meet another unknown interrogator. This man wanted quick and clear answers to his urgent question of the day. His English was terrible and I could not believe what I was being asked.

He demanded to know what a "muddy field" was. The Vietnamese military have very little understanding of electrical machinery. This man knew that an electromotive force had an E-field and a magnet had an H-field sometimes called a flux field. However, was uncertain how a "muddy field" applied.

He possessed a captured operator's manual for a gas-powered generator which said it could be safely used in a muddy field. He was harsh and threatened immediate punishment if I failed to answer him. I was near exhaustion due to my swollen injury and general lack of medical attention. I did not want to give him a lesson in English. So I pretended to swoon.

I was surprised to find when I awoke that I had indeed passed out. However, the right side of my face was like hamburger. He had been sitting in a chair near my head and periodically kicking my face to awaken me. It seemed that he wanted a quick success to show his boss like the *"what is a mil"* guy.

I realized that being a POW was not for sissies. There were hazards around every corner. Survival required brinkmanship and caution. Slowly, I cleared up his confusion and asked to see a doctor. He ignored my request and lumbered out of the room, obviously disappointed with his discovery and the length of time it took him to get it. I was hauled back to my dank cell.

The Forth Day

Day four was no better. Another interrogator, also unknown, was assigned to get me to write the names of the members left in my home squadron. Our training stressed the hazard of writing anything for the captor. Once induced to writing you might become a regular source for them for propaganda. As indicated earlier, avoidance techniques included statements such as: "I'm too weak and need medical attention;" "I can't understand you," and "I'm not good with words etc." None of these are effective if the captor has a requirement from on high to see the progress of their interrogators. I resorted to stall as long as I could, then write some response so poorly or laced with misinformation that the interrogators was forced to rewrite it and put it in the file as my own. If anybody read it on the radio for propaganda purposes, it was obvious that it was a fake.

As detailed earlier, in our training we were told of a prisoner who was forced to write the names of remaining members of his squadron. He listed Dick Tracy, Captain Marvel, Flash Gordon and number of other comic book characters. The Vietnamese delegation to the Paris Peace talks read the names aloud to the assembly, illustrating how the American POWs were assisting them to end the war. They lost face when they heard the snickering of the American delegation. The POW defeated the captor's attempt to exploit him. I applied the same misinformation technique with the interrogator on day four.

I said, "Most of the young pilots are already shot down. Only the old majors remain".

"Okay", he said, "write down their names"'

I listed: Dizzy Dean, Babe Ruth, Stan Musial and all of the "old Majors" that came to mind. Satisfied, he shuffled off without further efforts to coerce me.

For a total of twenty days in New Guy Village my captors periodically hauled me in to the Blue Room for more inane requests for trivial information. Then one morning two guards hoisted me out of New Guy Village and located me in another section of Hoa Lo called Little Vegas. The cell blocks were name after Las Vegas Casinos such as Caesar's Palace, Harold's Club etc. I was dumped into a thatched-roof cell in The Golden Nugget. The cell was across from a bath house. No sooner had the guards left that I heard a Vietnamese turnkey guard talking broken English to an American prisoner. I sat up on my liter and peered out the small window in the door. Surprised, I saw Captain Dewey Wayne Waddle, a pilot from my Squadron who had been shot down earlier. I waited until the turnkey had time to move away for other duties, then I said out loud, "I'm Major Mo Baker, Thud jock from the 357th Takhli, shot down 23 August, broken femur, on a litter."

I started through a repeat but stopped when I heard a loud cough. I took it as a warning signal that the turnkey was approaching. I was correct. The turnkey brought another POW to the bathing booths.

When he left, I heard Waddle say in a normal voice "Hi Mo, Its Wayne."

I responded with two coughs. I settled back on the litter with a smile. Wayne knew I had arrived and the grapevine would soon be informed of the new arrival. That was a good day. It seemed the initial interrogation phase had ended and I had begun the long-term day-to-day existence of a POW. The accommodations were horrible but dry, and the food was meager but edible. Although, I discovered the rats occupied the thatched-roof overhead; it could be worse, I mused. I'm not in chains yet.

My Cellmate, Larry Carrigan

The following morning the door opened in my cell and the turnkey inserted another prisoner who would be my cellmate-- Captain Larry E. Carrigan, an F-4 driver from Tempe, Arizona.

Larry graduated from Arizona State University before entering flight school. He had amassed 800 hours of jet time by the time he entered the war, leaving behind his wife, Sue, and three children Lorri, Steve, and Keith. He was an aircraft commander (front-seater) of an F-4 with the 555th TFS at Ubon RTAB, Thailand. A published account of his shoot-down complied by Task Force Omega recounts the details.

At 1335 hours on 23 August 1967, Major Charles R. Tyler, pilot, and Ronald N. Sittner, weapons systems officer, comprised the crew of an F-4D, call sign *Ford 01,* which departed Ubon Airfield as lead aircraft in a flight of four. Captain Larry E. Carrigan, pilot, and Capt. Charles Lane Jr.; weapons systems officer; comprised the crew of the number four aircraft, call sign *Ford 04.*

Ford flight conducted a strike mission on Yen Vien railroad yard located in a densely populated and heavily defended area approximately 36 miles north of Hanoi. Weather conditions consisted of scattered and towering cumulus over nearby Thud Ridge. The cloud bases were at 15,000 feet and the pilots had clear visibility during their afternoon mission.

At 1515 hours, while ingressing their target, the flight was attacked from the rear by a flight of two MiG-21s armed with air-to-air missiles (AAMs). In the ensuing dogfight, *Ford 04* was struck by an AAM and *Ford 01* was struck by another AAM immediately afterward. Other pilots in the flight saw three parachutes leave the two fireballs. Within minutes of the shoot down, other flight members heard three strong emergency beepers and one weak beeper. Voice contact was established with Larry Carrigan, the pilot of *Ford 04.*

The report continued to say that Major Tyler was captured immediately by ground forces and Captain Carrigan was captured by villagers after escaping and evading for three and a half days. Neither Sittner nor Lane every appeared in the POW camps and are assumed to have died at the hands of the enemy.

Larry reported that during his initial interrogation he attempted to use a cover story to explain why he was trekking through the jungle when discovered. He told his captors he was just a cargo pilot who wandered off course and crashed in their country by mistake. The story folded when two guards brought in an F-4 canopy with the name, Captain Larry Carrigan, painted on the lower rail.

Larry was shocked. He was not actually flying his signature aircraft the day he was shot down. Captain Robert Sawhill was assigned to fly his bird that day. Sawhill was not even in Ford flight. We later found out that Sawhill and crew had hydraulic failure while on a separate strike mission on 23 August 1967 and had to eject over enemy territory. They were captured and joined the ranks of American POWs in North Vietnam.

The Hospital

Mr. Peepers, a country doctor with coke-bottle lenses, squatted beside my litter poking at my injured left thigh. Through an interpreter he reported that, although badly swollen from the abuse during initial interrogation, the leg could be saved and pinned together. There was a provision, of course, that I cooperate with the prison authorities by telling them anything they needed to know. Abruptly he left. I breathed a sigh of relief to hear that my leg was salvageable.

The top interrogator, The Bug, had told me that if the leg rots, "we throw you away with it."

I believed him. He was not making idle threats. Out of 601 returnees from the *Hanoi Hilton*, no amputees returned. The Vietnamese simply did not want the trouble of caring for a maimed or severely injured POW.

After three weeks of interrogation and beatings at sporadic, unpredictable hours of the day or night, I was able to avoid supplying the enemy any significant information about my squadron or their attack tactics. Finally, four men lugged me out of the Hoa-Lo Prison, stuffed me into a six-by truck and secretly transported me to the Bach Mai Hospital in downtown Hanoi. The move was made under the cover of darkness in the wee hours of the morning to avoid civilian contact with the American.

As with so many historic structures in Vietnam, the Bach Mai Hospital was built by the French in 1911 and has, as one of its vistas, the railway line which runs north to the Chinese border and south to what was known as Saigon in 1968. Today the world calls it Ho-Chi-Minh City. The operating rooms were located underground and were lit by oil lamps—much more crude conditions than what was standard with even the most primitive American hospital. Incidentally, on December 22, 1972, a string of bombs intended for nearby Bach Mai Airfield hit the hospital, killing twenty-eight staff members. It was into this historic old structure that I was silently shuffled that morning.

Entering the back door to the hospital we were observed by an old man on a crutch dragging a badly damaged leg. Obviously a bomb victim, he rushed forward in an effort to crush my skull with a giant swing of his heavy crutch. A militia woman with drawn bayonet joined his threatening move. My litter bearers shouted them down and quickly put me inside.

I was placed on a cot in a small room that had a door on one end and two French-doors at the other end. To secure my makeshift quarters, a cotton rope was tied around the two handles of the French-doors. Newspaper was pasted over the glass panes in an attempt to hide me from public view. The guards left me alone in the room with a pillow and a tin cup of water before retiring to their own quarters.

Later that night I heard the *flap-zzz, flap-zzz* noise of the old man dragging his mangled limb towards my room. Noiselessly, he turned the knob to the single door near my head and leaned against the lock. I poised for the attack, armed only with a pillow and a tin cup for my defense. My heart pounded as I watched the doorknob being tried over and over again. The make-shift cotton rope lock held firm. Then the *flap-zzz, flap-zzz* of the old man's gait faded down the hall.

I felt as if I was in a Friday night horror movie. I remained wide awake the rest of the night, wondering what the other bomb victims were plotting, staring at the simple cotton rope securing the two French doors at my feet. I wondered how long the rope could delay the intruders on the other side of the doors.

At dawn the locked door near my head was attacked with violent force. This time loud voices swore at their inability to enter.

An alternate plan was being devised. With a crash the French-doors were pushed inward putting a strain on the cotton rope which secured the handles. Through the crack between the doors I could see the face of the angry militia woman. Instantly, she inserted her bayonet and severed the rope. She stepped in the room waving her bayonet before my pillow and cup. Then she stepped to one side to allow a slender, white-coated doctor to enter. With some amusement he explained in French that they had broken the key off in the door and he had to ask the militia woman to assist them getting into my room. I gasped for air; my pulse was racing.

The surgeon was kind and concerned about my injury. With his broken English and polished French he explained the nature of the injury and the repair procedure. He gave orders to have me prepared for surgery the following dawn. To the credit of the medical profession, the surgeon was never hostile and treated me as any other wounded soldier that needed his care. The corpsman, however, was a different story. He was extremely hostile and looked for ways to inflict pain on the American whenever possible.

The prep-for-surgery bath was an opportunity for the corpsman to demonstrate his great disdain for the *Yankee air-pirate*, which he cruelly did for the benefit and amusement of a dozen nurse-aids and bystanders. He had me removed to a large latrine and placed on the floor. With a water hose attached to the cold faucet he played the stream of water over my naked, shivering body while he joked and bantered with the tittering crowd. Then he scraped at the hair on my leg and pubic area with bold, flourishing strokes of an open-bladed razor, leaving crimson bloody scratches marking his progress. The crowd alternately grimaced and snickered.

At dawn he wheeled me to the operating room, placed me on the stainless-steel table, and gleefully splashed the harsh disinfectant on the fresh cuts and scratches. When the surgeon arrived moments later he frowned at the corpsman's maltreatment of his patient, asking *"Who is supposed to be the surgeon here."* The corpsman smirked and left the doctor and anesthetist to do their tasks. After the spinal block took effect, they repaired the leg with a femoral pin and lashed the limb to a straight board.

Apparently, the doctor gave orders to leave the American alone. I was not threatened again. A few days later the stitches were removed and a clumsy plaster cast was applied. The following three weeks I was allowed to rest and recuperate. To pass the time I applied the mind-occupying methods recommended by survival school. They suggested that we mentally build a dream home or boat, mentally work out difficult problems, or mentally compose a song or novel. I mentally recalled all of the mathematical techniques of Calculus I and II. Then one night I was whisked out of the hospital back to the prison.

Chapter 5
DAYS AS AN AMERICAN POW

After the initial interrogation phase of my captivity and a thirty-day stay at Bach Mai Hospital, I entered the routine life of a POW in the hands of the North Vietnamese Communists. We were not regarded as Prisoners of War but rather as *black criminals that deserve to be shot.* The Vietnamese reminded us often that if it were not for the *humane and lenient* policies of Ho Chi Minh we would have been executed upon capture.

We were not deceived. As indicated earlier, we were aware that there were three good reasons for an enemy to retain prisoners. First, the captor gained military information that may be useful for the short term. Secondly, the captor used the prisoners for propaganda proposes if they could be intimidated into making antiwar statements. Lastly, the captor used the detainees for trading pawns at the close of hostilities.

Communication By Means Of The Tap Code

Just prior to my departure to the Bac Mai Hospital, Carrigan and I were relocated to *The Plantation*, an old French colonialist manor surrounded by rows of cells and high stonewalls topped with broken glass and barbed wire. We immediately made contact with the other POWs and began to learn things that POWs should know. We were informed who was the Senior Ranking Officer

(SRO), what his resistance policies were, and his stand on accepting early release.

We learned the names of every known POW and, most important of all, *The Tap Code*. The Tap Code was a system of tapping on the walls to communicate with anyone who could hear. The system was brought into the POW camps by Smitty Carlyle Harrison, a prisoner shot down early in the conflict. Smitty had learned this code in his survival training prior to the war. This easy-to-learn system was the single-most beneficial element of our resistance to the enemy's attempt to divide and conquer the POW population.

The flexibility of the Tap Code was excellent, because it was so simple. It was easy to learn. You whispered to the new guy the description of the code and asked him to scribe it onto a bar of soap. If the Vietnamese came in the POW just whisked it off and then practiced on it overnight and in the morning if he was required to tap the wall, he could do it. It didn't take long to learn. Or he could do it holding the bar of soap in front of him providing a visual of the letters. At first it might be slow but he could do it.

Imagine a five-by-five array of letters of the alphabet. Omit the letter *K*. Use a *C* instead. The first row is *ABCDE*, then *FGHIJ*, then and *LMNOP* etc. Simply tap the row and column of the letter, pausing slightly between the row and columns. For example the letter *B* is tapped TAP - TAP TAP. This code is superior to the Morse code because dashes cannot be tapped on the wall. We used the familiar cadence of *shave-and-a-hair-cut* for a call-up signal with *two-bits* as an acknowledging response.

Despite the strict rules against communication with other cells or prisoners, we communicated at every opportunity, keeping each other advised on the enemy's tactics and sharing any knowledge we had on any subject. It was our belief that if another prisoner risks a beating to ask you a question about, say, the difference between a sugar mule and a cotton mule, you must take the same risk to find the information. The information might have great importance to the one asking or at least serve to keep his mind occupied and sane during the long-term duress that we were experiencing. I spent countless hours with my ear pressed against the cold stone walls of our cell, listening to the faint tapping of neighboring POWs expanding the confinement of my cell to the lives of everybody in camp.

We had a lot of flexibility of whether you're tapping walls, sweeping leaves, or snapping a towel. One individual was isolated into a little small building out in the courtyard, at the Zoo I'm told. He actually didn't have a wall to tap to because he was in a stand-alone building out in the courtyard. And, yet he could get up in the morning and snap his towel—we all had a wash rag of our own. He would do it in such a manner that he could report to his fellow prisoners that he was in good shape and that the Vietnamese were asking him for a false confession or whatever he had to communicate.

From building to building we found also you could slip a little white piece of paper which is visible underneath the door and the other buildings could see that. And, then you could slip a response. It's a silent code going across the courtyard for sixty or seventy feet. You could do it with the guard present. And, if you had just a little bit of a blind between the guard and your little piece of paper, you could do it all day and the guard could be standing right there.

I recall at Son Tay there was one individual in the *Cathouse* who was an English major. He kindly sent us a quatrain of poetry everyday just to keep us entertained and lift our spirits from the days of endless boredom. We all learned, "East is east and West is west..." which by my understanding is Rudyard Kipling's "The Ballad of East and West." It was also my understanding it has forty-seven quatrains in it. I do know that it takes twenty minutes to recite. It took him forty-seven days to send it using the Tap Code.

The same kind of thing happened between the walls with the Tap Code. So goes communication, so goes morale. It was the most important activity we did for each other while we were in the prison camp. Our obligation was, man for man, to help the guy on the other side of the wall anytime he has a problem. If he sent through a message saying, "I'm out of my mind with boredom; send details on WWII." We would start on WWII from the beginning.

In fact, that was one of the messages that came through the wall. And, collectively, we sent him all the details we had. After months we had expended our collective knowledge to the bored prisoner, we asked him what else did he need? He sent a follow-up message that just said, "Send details." His mind was at stake here, so all of us would dream up items to send to him so he did not feel alone. We realized that communication was one of the strongest things we had going for us. The flexibility of the Tap Code was amazing.

We invented better ways to utilize the Tap Code. The POWs in the courtyard, visible to other cells, could finger the code by extending one to five fingers in Tap Code cadence. Seaman Apprentice Douglas Hegdhal was not considered a POW but rather a seaman lost at sea (he actually fell off the ship.) Because he was not regarded as a *black criminal*, he was allowed to sweep leaves off the walkways within the courtyard. Although only nineteen years old at the time, he cleverly swept code as he worked.

The swish-swish rhythms of his broom went unnoticed by the guards. He bravely relayed messages that we whispered to him to other rooms across camp. He was willing to help anybody despite the hazard of severe punishment if he were caught communicating.

Two recent captives, Bob Craner and Guy Gruters who were members of a crew shot down in the DMZ flying the F-100 *Misty* missions. These two men were moved into a cell adjacent to Larry and me at the Plantation. Whispering late at night under the cell doors, we explained the Tap Code and told them to contact us on our common wall with a *shave-and-haircut* call-up signal the next day. At dawn we answered an excited call-up signal from the new guys' cell with the *two-bits* response.

They tapped as if they had been practicing all night saying, "There is a spider in here that you wouldn't believe. Its webbing spreads all across the door. WHAT TO DO?"

All insects in the tropics are huge. The camp was full of fearsome looking, but harmless, garden spiders that measured eight inches across and spun heavy, sticky thread. More alarming was their ability to jump six feet without warning.

"Run for your lives!" we tapped.

"Get serious," they said. "I mean this baby could eat birds! WHAT TO DO?"

"Sacrifice a virgin," we advised and left them to deal with the spider like big boys.

But, beyond the point of communicating for instruction, guidance, and compassion, the Tap Code served an important role in establishing a POW's existence among the ranks. There is much solace and comfort in knowing your people knew you were there and were working to get you home. The first step in doing that was to get your name out.

The Tap Code was crucial in getting a name out. It was a requirement for all of the prisoners of war to learn the entire list of all the names that we knew were prisoners. We also taught those to Seaman Hegdhal because it looked like they were going to release him for propaganda purposes. It was no fault of his that he'd fallen off his ship, and he was given permission by the Senior Ranking Officer to go if it was offered him.

We were going to try to get Hegdhal a roommate who knew the entire list and slowly we would be able to teach him the list. Since the North Vietnamese assigned roommates as they saw fit, this was not going to be a particularly easy task. However, the Senior Ranking Officer passed the word to have Hegdhal tell his captor he was lonely and wished to have a roommate. Amazingly, the North Vietnamese saw him as being harmless and consented to his wish.

They could have selected any of us to be his roommate. However, totally by chance Joe Crecca was assigned, and Crecca got the entire list into his head. Seaman Hegdhal took that list of names home with him. On the list were people who the government didn't know were alive or dead--nor did their loved ones. It was an excellent opportunity to get those names out to them. That was a primary reason for communication: to see who was there and who was alive, including those POWs located in any of the other camps.

Communication was the saving grace for the sanity of those required to live alone. With daily contact with some other miserable soul, somehow life became more bearable. This was particularly true during the bombing halt from 1968 to 1972. For four years the American prisoners waited through long hours of boredom in the hot cells, biding their time until the US decided to bring an end to its part in the Vietnamese struggle.

No doubt the solidarity enjoyed by the POWs, the one-for all, all-for-one spirit, was directly due to the Tap Code and our indomitable efforts to keep communication alive regardless of the punishment. Today all military survival training schools teach the communication techniques we perfected in Vietnam. I pray that they will never need them

"Brainwashing"

After the initial interrogation period the interaction between guard and prisoner changed from torture to sustained indoctrination, or brainwashing. Merriam-Webster dictionary provides the following definition of brainwashing: "a forcible indoctrination to induce someone to give up basic political, social, or religious beliefs and attitudes and to accept contrasting regimented ideas." Quite simply, the North Vietnamese wanted us to sympathize with their condition and rebuff the actions of the American policy in Vietnam. They didn't simply want us to "see it their way" they wished us to believe as they did. To that end our captors continuously interviewed and preached to the POWs on an individual basis.

The North Vietnamese Communists were persistent and comprehensive, insisting on brainwashing everybody. They spent endless hours brainwashing their own subjects. Daily they met to praise the clear-eyed leadership of Ho Chi Minh and the communist party. It was natural for the prison authorities to have a weekly conference with each prisoner to present their view of the world, the war, and their cause. Their pitch was invariable and followed a set party line which was:

1. *The war against the Vietnamese people is illegal.* The Vietnamese people never even threw a stone at the American shores.

2. *The war is immoral.* America is raping Vietnam for its tin and tungsten.

3. *The war is unjust.* How can such a superpower like America justify brutally bombing a small country like Vietnam?

Once a week the turnkey guard would come to our cell and call for one of us to put on our long set of prison pajamas. The prisoner was then led to the big house for a three-hour session on the lesson of the week. The training room was furnished with very few items: a table covered with a blue cloth, a desk lamp, a chair and fan for the interrogator, and a low, three-legged stool for the prisoner. As if staged by a low-budget Hollywood movie, the prisoner was spotlighted with the desk lamp and caused him to sit at a lower level than the superior captor.

Struggling with the English, the interrogator droned through two to three hours of prepared propaganda on the Vietnamese legal, moral and just position in the war. The reader was rarely well educated but rather chosen because he could speak mediocre English. The pilots on the other hand were all college graduates and well trained in the communists' approach to brainwashing. The North Vietnamese were never successful or convincing in their efforts.

The brainwashing sessions were dangerous, however. A show of animosity, belligerence, or even impoliteness might incur a severe beating or extended solitaire confinement. Our resistance to the training sessions took other forms. One prisoner was skilled at leaning slowly to one side until he was nearly forty-five degrees. The reader found himself leaning also in order to deliver the message. He repeatedly had to stop the session and straighten everybody up.

Another prisoner occupied himself with stalking flies or mosquitoes; interrupting the session with sudden smacks on his arm or leg followed by triumphantly counting and gloating over his kills.

Chasing Rabbits

My favorite diversionary tactic was to lead the reader far away from the subject. For example, one week the reader had to give three hours of dogma on "The Woman's' Role in the Peoples' Republic."

After his introduction of the subject I said, "Good, I need to know how boy meets girl in your country."

Indignantly, he responded, "You must not meet a woman. You are a *black criminal*."

"I don't mean me. I mean you. How do you meet a woman in Vietnam such as that girl out there?" I corrected, pointing to a female soldier walking by the window.

Spotting the girl he looked shocked and stammered, "I must not meet that girl! She is the camp commander's girl friend."

The camp commander took a siesta daily with that particular squeeze dolly.

"All right then," I continued, "some other girl for example. How do you get to meet her?"

"Perhaps I send her a note," he replied thoughtfully.

"That's good," I replied, noticing his blush and then continued, "I used that technique in grammar school a lot. What does the note say? Does it say 'I love you? Do you love me? Check yes. Check no?'"

"No, no," he insisted, "I would say, 'If it pleases you we can take the tea and cookies together Sunday afternoon.'"

Having very little rank he was offering to spend his entire weekly allowance of *six hou five soo*, about sixty-five cents, on her.

"Very nice," I said approvingly, "And no doubt you will take the tea and cookies by the lake and watch the beautiful swans glide by. Since you bought the tea and cookies, do you get to hold her hand or put your arm around her?"

"I don't think so," he answered, squirming a little because he didn't like the direction the conversation was going.

"Okay," I persisted, "next Sunday you spring for another round of tea and cookies. Do you get to put your arm around her then?"

"Perhaps," he admitted.

"Do you get to squeeze her bosom?" I ventured.

"NO!" he shouted. "That would be very bad behavior."

"I know, I know," I agreed, calming him a bit. "It is the same in my country. If my mother sees me do it she will slap my face."

"You have a wise mother!" he huffed.

"But, we do it anyway, don't you?" I offered.

"Yeah," he admitted, looking at the floor somewhat embarrassed.

For the next hour we continued the conversation until he and his hypothetical girl friend were behind the bushes doing the X-rated activities all cultures do. At the end of the session, he wrote in his report book "Baker understands the Women's Role in the Peoples Republic."

The Marvel of Eight-Hundred Dollars

The brightest interrogators were not immune from being diverted from their subjects. Once I was summoned to listen to a civilian from the higher echelons of the political system. He sought to both evaluate the camp commander's brainwashing progress on the prisoners and teach them the political views of the Party of The People (communist).

I interrupted him immediately saying, "You speak excellent English. You could be an interpreter at the United Nations translating your statesmen's speeches into English. Those people make eight hundred dollars a month."

"Hmm," he said with his interest piqued, "Is that a lot of money?"

"Let me tell you what you could afford for eight hundred dollars a month," I responded. "You could afford a bicycle for every member of the family."

He had borrowed a bicycle to journey to the camp for this interview. His eyes widened as I continued.

"You could have furniture in the house for people to sit on. No need to sit on the floor. You could have toilets that flush and go 'swoosh' instead of the 'bomb sight' types with the drop tanks under them. You could buy a new suit or a new dress for your wife every month. You could drink a beer every night with your evening meal."

I plunged on with the wonderful life eight hundred dollars a month would provide. He was fascinated, transfixed, and hypnotized for the rest of the session while I brainwashed him on the wonders of the capitalist system.

The ploy worked so well that when he returned to the camp the following month for another session, instead of selecting another prisoner at random he told the camp authority to bring me to him. As soon as I was seated he asked, "What else can I get for my eight hundred dollars?"

111

Some interrogation sessions were aimed at gaining hard information to go into our folder to show the *High Office* the interrogation program was being executed well by this camp. We had been cautioned in our training schools to not get into confrontations with the enemy over these issues if the requested information was not secret or could nor its veracity able to be confirmed by the enemy.

The North Vietnamese *High Office* insisted also that prisoners supply information on all of their family and important political officials. Naturally, we falsified that data. However, every year our captors attempted to verify the data on the biography. The biographies never matched. Each year we insisted that the latest version was the correct one. After the fourth or fifth iteration they abandoned gathering biographies.

On one occasion I was pressured to reveal what secondary duties I had at the air base in Thailand. Our captors were aware the pilots had college degrees and usually took additional duties on the bases other than flying. I convinced them that I was in charge of the sewage ditches, which seemed reasonable to them since their raw sewage flows in open ditches throughout the villages. I described cutting ditches around the Officers' Club, down around the end of the runway where the Colonel's cornfield was, through the Thai housing area and back to the big ditch that passes outside of the main gate. Somewhere in Vietnam there is a portfolio on me which includes a sketch of *The Big Finger* I made of the sewage ditches.

It was war every day in the prison for the American POWs. The North Vietnamese wanted us to denounce the war effort and our leaders. They sought to gain propaganda from us in every way. They wanted us to write false confessions. They wanted us to make tapes to be broadcast on the Hanoi radio urging other warriors to lay down their weapons. They wanted to film us receiving huge feasts at Christmas, which they would not allow to be eaten. They wanted us to visit with Jane Fonda or other peaceniks to provide propaganda against the war. We took torture to avoid aiding and abetting the enemy.

We considered that our mission in captivity was to keep a low profile, survive, give the enemy no aid through our actions or words, and to one day return with our personal and national honor intact. Our stated motto was "Return With Honor."

The communists failed to convert a single American pilot to their view. Years and years of brainwashing efforts were fruitless. The returning POWs were still Red, White, and Blue to their shorts, proudly saluting the flag and eager to return to duty.

I believe history will record that although they were confined like animals and treated like animals, the American POWs served their country like real men during those dark years.

POW Treatment in the Camps

As I provide detailed accounts of my experiences during the time of my captivity among the different camps, it is crucial to revisit the established policy of the Democratic Republic of North Vietnam (DRNV) toward captured American flyers. The Vietnamese did not recognize the Geneva Conventions of 1954 because, in their view, the US was a foreign aggressor interfering in the Vietnamese Civil War.

As I have stated time and again, Ho Chi Minh insisted the American flyers, who were shot down over North Vietnam, were criminals. In fact they were *black criminals, air pirates* who did not warrant mercy of any sort. They were considered on the same social strata as murderers, rapists, drug dealers, and villains of the most heinous kind. There was no justice for them. They were subject to and worthy of any sort of brutality or torture which could be imagined by their captors. Therefore, any treatment short of execution given to the American prisoners was due to the *humane and lenient treatment of the North Vietnamese people.*

And although this may seem to be repetitive material to the reader, it was a policy and litany which was continuously and monotonously drilled into the captive airman for the duration of his captivity. Read any account of a POW's captivity and the same words and phrases attributed to the enemy will most assuredly be repeated.

Accordingly, every camp or prison which housed American POWs was fair game to whatever torture or treatment was deemed justified by their handlers. There have been some who have suggested not all confinement experienced by the POWs was as equally severe as others, implying that some of the POWs did not have it so bad due to the place where they spent their captivity. While it is true that some of the camps were particularly brutal, none of the camps--not a one was an easy stay.

Torture, mistreatment, and brutality existed at every prison and was doled out with equal fervor at the pleasure and whim of our captors. The initial interrogation, which occurred on the immediate days following capture, was always, in every case and in whatever camp, brutal and literally torturous.

To bicker and fuss over which level of brutality was considered worse and in which camp is to this day an insult to the brave men who were subjected to whatever level of torture dealt out by the thugs of the Democratic Republic of North Vietnam, on any level. However, there was a marked difference in the level of brutality experienced by all POWs before and after the death of Ho Chi Minh.

Atheists in Foxholes

In one of our past wars, someone asserted that there are no atheists in foxholes. The remark implies that at a moment when death seems probable, American soldiers, whether atheist or devotees of a religion, suddenly become avid worshipers of God, praying for forgiveness of their sins and asking for delivery from the hands of the enemy--nonsense! The American fighting man carries his religion into battle whether he realizes it or not. By the very nature of our American heritage *Under God* we are all aware of some very fundamental notions about religion that give us enormous advantage over our enemies in battle or captivity. Let me explain.

In my generation, by the time American children entered the first grade of elementary school, they became aware of certain basics in monotheism. Their parents, Sunday school teachers, siblings and neighborhood playgroups taught them:

A. *There is a God, a supreme being that is all-powerful, all-knowing and ever-present.*

B. *That God knows them and they are important to Him.*

C. *That they may communicate with Him through prayer.*

These simple concepts were fundamental to our culture and most American children had them firmly internalized by their first school year.

To be sure, not all American soldiers were regular attendees of church but all of them knew how to employ their right of communication with their God when the occasion demanded it. I have observed first-hand men asking for God's protection in battle who have not darkened the Chapel door since their marriage but who have felt perfectly natural and comfortable in prayer before battle. And, well they should! Ours is a nation *Under God* and we are not ashamed of it.

In 1967 the Vietnamese culture under the communists allowed religion but they were very careful not to let the clergy have too much influence. Most of our captors, particularly the enlisted men, had little or no concept of God, the hereafter, or prayer. Their national heritage in this area was a loosely bound package of superstitions that addressed certain rules of good behavior: such as incest, thievery and murder, but very little else. Their idea of Heaven was a vague concept of a spiritual existence

115

in some other dimension where their ancestors reside and observe their deeds. Thus, they are supposed to behave well while on earth to make their family ancestors proud.

The concept of prayer, on the other hand was quite strange to them. They snickered at the Americans knelling and praying as well as our Sunday worship services. Wisely, the leadership of our captors advised the guards not to get into conversations about religion with the Americans because the Americans might become highly agitated or even violent about it.

The communists were not above taking advantage of our need to worship for their own purposes of propaganda. To this end in December of 1968 our captors announced to my cellmate, Larry Carrigan, and me that there would be a worship service Christmas Eve and we would be allowed to attend. There would be a civilian preacher, music and a communion service. However, since members of other camps might be attending, we must not talk to anyone while in the service. Preventing the POWs from communicating was not likely to happen unless a Vietnamese guard separated each prisoner. We agreed to attend.

At the designated hour, when darkness assisted them in their policy of keeping prisoners from visual contact, Carrigan and I were led to a meeting hall which had on many occasions served as a torture room. We were seated next to other prisoners and advised to "Keep silence!" As soon as the guard went for the next pair of prisoners, we began talking to the other POWs. We learned that they were from another camp South of Hanoi known as *The Zoo*. These men had been POWs for two or more years. They had seen this Christmas routine before. They told us there would be cameras grinding when the service started.

About this time an American voice spoke from the back of the POW group as if he were making and important announcement.

He shared, "This camp is known as *the Plantation*. The Senior Ranking Officer is Colonel Ted Guy. There are fifty-seven POWs confined here. Prepare to copy."

Then the speaker spoke each Plantation POW's name in alphabetical order. It was an amazing display of audacity and courage. Memory experts in the crowd from the other camps memorized the names and reported them to their own Senior Ranking Officer (SRO) the next day.

This intra-camp communication made attendance to the Christmas service worthwhile although the enemy used the film for propaganda in the coming year to improve the Vietnamese image in the world's opinion. The film release touted the *humane and lenient treatment* being given the Americans confined in Vietnam. We attempted to invalidate their claims by presenting the third finger to the camera when it was pointed in our direction. American intelligence agencies made use of the film for identification of POWs not yet known to be alive and well.

A Vietnamese Episcopal pastor conducted the 1968 service. However, the pastor spoke no English. The communist interrogator, known to us as *Soft Soap Fairy*, translated the Pastor's remarks and added a bit of communist party line in the process. For example, he translated one passage thus:

> *The People's revolutionary hero, Jesus of Nazareth, a member of the working class, rose up against the Imperialist Roman tyrants. He inspired the people to form a liberation force to overthrow the tyrants. He was martyred at the hands of the evil imperialists.*

The music for the ceremony consisted of the pastor singing a hymn *a cappella* in Vietnamese. He sang, "There is a Fountain Filled with Blood" while a POW passed around the bread and wine sacraments. The wine was actually orange liquor supplied by the pastor. The POW sitting next to me gulped his tiny portion of liquor and said, "Man! I need a quart of this blood."

On Christmas Day, our captors fed the prisoners a full meal. Only four occasions per year merited a meal of bread, meat, and vegetables: Christmas, Thanksgiving, Ho Chi Minh's birthday, and Tet, the Oriental New Year.

Interestingly, the day after the holiday the friendliness of our captors disappeared. All smiling and politeness ended. The guards resumed their duties and we resumed ours.

There were occasions when the Americans exploited the enemy's lack of knowledge about prayer. From time to time the Vietnamese interrogator lost patience with the *bad attitude* of a POW who would not sit quietly and listen to the propaganda lesson of the week. On those occasions the interrogator often sentenced the POW to spend the night in handcuffs.

The handcuffs were poorly constructed and of low quality. They were similar to the toy store handcuffs we had as kids when playing *Cops and Robbers*. A locking pall rested in a notched edge of the handcuff. Most POWs found that by inserting a straw from our rice mat that served as our sleeping pad, the pall would release. POWs rarely spent the night in handcuffs. Usually the POW would put the cuffs back on by the time the guards made their rounds in the morning.

One prisoner who was caught out of his handcuffs early one rainy, stormy morning was immediately hauled before the camp commander.

"Who released you from your handcuffs?" he demanded.

"God did." The POW answered.

"God? How you get God to do it?" he queried.

"Easy," the POW answered. "I prayed about it." The POW reverently placed his hands together in prayer and bowed his head.

"I am the only one who can give the order to release you from your handcuffs." The Officer huffed.

"But, God looks after us." retorted the POW, pointing upward.

As heaven would have it, at that very moment a bolt of lightning struck near the interrogation room, shaking the foundations of the building with the accompanying thunder.

The Camp Commander jumped to his feet wide-eyed and shouted, "Go back to your room. AND NO MORE PRAYING."

The power of prayer is far more potent than most people realize. When the Vietnamese camp commander wished to punish one of his own soldiers, he would place him out of communications and sight of the other soldiers. Those soldiers were miserable and alone because they had no one with whom to interact or turn to.

Such was not the case with the Americans. When I was given solitary confinement, I was never alone. I was merely separated from my fellow POWs but always in the company of my God. I had long conversations with God who gave me great comfort and satisfaction. Often I was able to sort out some thorny personal problems which I had been intending to give serious thought to for years.

When my sentence of solitary confinement ended, I happily returned to my fellow POWs. My captors could not understand why I was not demoralized but rather refreshed and ready to return to my regular activities. The power of prayer is a national heritage that each American carries into battle. It has awesome capabilities and advantages over the Godless enemy.

We never attempted to convert the guards to our religion but they were very curious and observant when we worshiped. They were aware that every Sunday morning someone sounded an artificial, loud sneeze, signaling the beginning of the hour of worship. It was our custom for all of the POWs to worship at the same time, although we were forbidden to be in the same place. One could hear humming and singing of familiar hymns seeping out of the closed cells. Carrigan and I remained in complete silence for the hour of worship.

It was our time to talk with God or to mentally visit with our families. These were emotional times and very, very private. I have seen the toughest; hardened warriors shed tears for their loved ones during these moments. The Sunday morning worship hour was a necessary and fulfilling ritual that was practiced by every American that I knew in the POW camps of North Vietnam.

Our greatest opportunity to show the Godless enemy the true nature of our religious culture came November 1970 when suddenly the American POWs were gathered from the outlying camps and assembled at Hoa Lo Prison in downtown Hanoi. The Air Force Special Forces had raided a small camp in the countryside at Son Tay.

Although no Americans were there in that particular camp at that particular time, the Vietnamese realized that security of the American prisoners could only be assured in the downtown dungeon of Hoa Lo, which we called the "Hanoi Hilton, which I have already established was far from being a hotel with its walls of two-foot thick stone. It was cold and nasty. It was filled with large wharf-size rats that roamed the camp day or night.

However, the *Hilton* did hold one advantage for us. For the first time the Americans were placed in large rooms of forty men more or less. We had suffered confinement in one and two-man rooms for years, but at the *Hilton* at this time, we had forty roommates to enjoy.

The 400 or so American prisoners arriving at Hoa Lo quickly organized into a military structure. The Senior Ranking Officer of each room was identified. He then organized the men into four flights led by the ranking officer of each flight. Work groups and activities were organized. Volunteers stepped forward to lead the Sunday Hour of Worship.

The very first Sunday a loud, artificial sneeze initiated the worship in the ten large rooms. In our room, Room Three, Bill Butler served as the music director. He formed a quartet to sing the prayer responses and present an anthem. I was a part of that choir since I had been singing tenor in a choir from age fifteen. Our music was tasteful and reverent. We were all elated that we were going to be able to worship without cameras grinding away making propaganda.

Monday morning, however, the doors to the huge confinement room opened and three guards demanded that I put on my long pajamas and come with them. The requirement to wear the long pajamas usually meant that the prisoner was going to be presented to a high-ranking authority. I was led to the interrogation room known to us as the *Blue Room* where many of us had received our initial interrogation and torture. I was presented to the Camp Commander known to us as the *Rat*.

Sternly, the Rat said, "My guards tell me you have the most beautiful voice"

"Well, I…" I stammered, realizing what he meant. It was not a compliment. When the Vietnamese camp commander assembled his soldiers for their weekly dose of indoctrination, they started the meeting with inspirational patriotic singing. The soldier with the most beautiful voice sang the first phrase to cue the group to the pitch and cadence. Then they all sang. The camp commander accused me of leading the men in Room Three in patriotic rally songs, perhaps to incite riot and revolt. No doubt the guards had recognized my tenor voice above the other members of the quartet.

"I have not given you permission to sing in the rooms." The Rat said.

"But these are religious songs that teach the men to be content with their conditions and have patience with their place. You see, it is good for you and good for the prisoners. If the men are calm and content, they will be well behaved and have the *good attitude*. If they are not allowed to worship, they may become discontent and have the *bad attitude*. Our religious ceremonies are not political. We talk only of our souls and the importance of having good behavior." I paused for the translator to catch up.

"All right, then!" he said in English, interrupting the interpreter.

I knew he understood a great deal of English. That's why I spoke slowly and used very simple words.

"But you must only sing on Sunday and you must be very quiet so the other rooms do not hear you. Understand?" he said.

I nodded and took my leave while I was ahead. Upon returning to Room Three, I reported to the SRO, Doug Clower the details of the meeting with The Rat. We met with the choir and told them the conditions for continuing the singing. Since it was me who was known as the *most beautiful voice* the choir saw no reason not to continue. As a matter of fact, Bill Butler, nicknamed Bulla, met Wednesday night with eight men for choir practice. At my expression of concern, Bulla said not to worry. Until one of us of got beat up, namely me, we would press on to bigger and better things.

Monday after Sunday's worship service, the camp commander called me upon the carpet again. He had the full report from his guards.

"You must have misunderstood me." He said. "My men saw you singing Wednesday evening and on Sunday they saw you singing with eight singers."

"Yes, but we were singing softly. And we sang songs of comfort and patience. It is good for the men and it is good for you. Notice that they all have the *good attitude?*" I answered uneasily.

After a thoughtful pause he spoke slowly. "Remember-- softly."

I returned to Room Three with the news. Everybody just shrugged at my report. They saw I was not beat up so apparently we were getting away with our music program. Since *the most beautiful voice* would catch the Rat's heat, Bill and the choir had no intention of letting up. They intended to go about their business of providing inspiration and entertainment with their music, even at my expense. I took solace in the Sermon on the Mount when the Lord said, "Blessed is he that suffers for my sake..." If I did start taking lumps over the music program, perhaps I would be gaining stars in my crown.

Bill Butler had a flair for music. As a matter of fact he taught music to Room Three with the use of our choir. He sketched a large piano board on the concrete floor with a roofing tile chard. Then he stood his singers on each key and hummed a note to remember. Then when he pointed to us we sounded our tone like a bell choir member ringing their one note. With his live keyboard he taught the men of Room Three about harmony and the tonic chords.

Unafraid of the camp commander, Bulla presented bigger and better musical treats. Our choir grew to a dozen singers. We presented musical effects during the weeknights when other members of Room Three were telling movies. Later, he presented a musical, **South Pacific**, without regard for volume or number of singers. The camp commander was fully aware of the extravaganza. Since the other nine rooms of POWs were pursuing their own entertainment programs as well, the Rat realized there were no political rallies going on. I was never called before the Rat again for upbraiding.

The culmination of Bill Butler's musical crusade was during the Christmas week of 1971. We had prepared the story of the birth of Christ in music. We passed the word to the camp commander that the Christmas Pageant was going to be presented Sunday night after the evening meal and they were invited to attend.

We sang for well over an hour, singing all the Christmas carols that told the Christmas story. We finished with Handel's **Halleluiah Chorus**, sung by forty men in full voice. High in the vents of our huge cell were the faces of perhaps fifteen or twenty Vietnamese officers and enlisted men. They leaned ladders up to wall and stacked boxes to reach the ten-foot high vents to peer into our cell. The Vietnamese observers cheered and clapped for us after the big finish.

I will never forget the triumphant moment that I shared with Bulla and the choirboys. I like to think we all earned a star or two in our crowns that Christmas for bringing a few atheists to our foxhole.

Chapter 6
The Camps

I was held captive as a prisoner of war for five-and-a-half years. As I recount the experiences endured during that period it may be difficult for some to keep up with the locations where I was held. As some read these experiences, it may seem as if I was held at a single location for the duration of my imprisonment. That is not the case. Counting the place where I was shot down, there are ten locations of significance during this period. These included five different prisoner of war camps, the hospital, the rice paddy in which I was shot down, and my final destination of Clark Field in the Philippines.

Prison Shuffle

I was whisked back and forth between these camps for reasons apparent only to my captors, apparently subject to the whim of a paranoid and political communist bureaucracy. Nevertheless, the largest portion of years were spent at what was known as the Plantation, with approximately 840 of my total 2030 days of captivity spent there. Even so, that only represented 41 % of my time. My next largest stay was at the Hoa Lo prison in Hanoi, also known as the Hanoi Hilton where I spent 430 of my days in captivity. Combined, the Plantation and the Hanoi Hilton accounted for 63% of my time as a prisoner of war of the communist government of North Vietnam. Interesting enough, my shortest stay was at the Bac Mai hospital in Hanoi, where I spent my first month. The remainder of time was spent in other camps relatively near Hanoi, with the exception of Dogpatch.

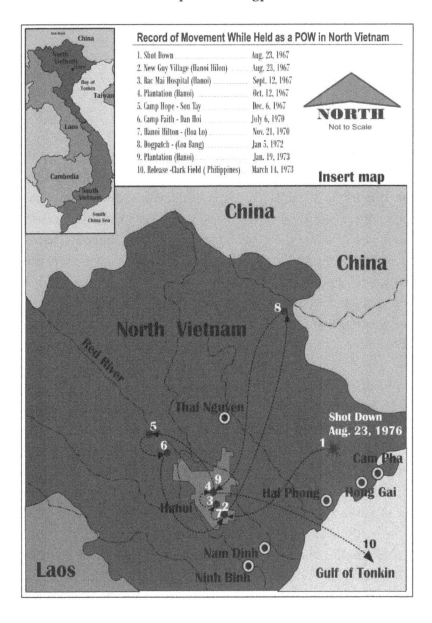

Record of Movement While Held as a POW in North Vietnam

1. Shot Down — Aug. 23, 1967
2. New Guy Village (Hanoi Hilton) — Aug. 23, 1967
3. Bac Mai Hospital (Hanoi) — Sept. 12, 1967
4. Plantation (Hanoi) — Oct. 12, 1967
5. Camp Hope - Son Tay — Dec. 6, 1967
6. Camp Faith - Dan Hoi — July 6, 1970
7. Hanoi Hilton - (Hoa Lo) — Nov. 21, 1970
8. Dogpatch - (Coa Bang) — Jan 5, 1972
9. Plantation (Hanoi) — Jan. 19, 1973
10. Release -Clark Field (Philippines) — March 14, 1973

Insert map

NORTH
Not to Scale

126

Days in Captivity According to Prison Camp

Place	Date In	Date Out	Total Days
Shot down	08/23/67	-	-
New Guy Village (Hoa Lo)	08/23/67	09/12/67	20
Bac Mai Hospital (Hanoi)	09/12/67	10/12/67	30
Plantation (Hanoi)	10/12/67	12/6/69	786
Camp Hope (Son Tay)	12/6/69	7/6/70	212
Camp Faith	07/6/70	11/21/70	138
Hanoi Hilton (Hoa Lo)	11/21/70	1/5/72	410
Dogpatch (Coa Bang)	01/5/72	01/19/73	380
Plantation (Hanoi)	01/19/73	03/14/73	54
Release to Clark Field	03/14/73 -		-
	Total days in captivity		2,030

The Plantation

Camp Plantation, also known as *the Citadel*, is in downtown Hanoi a few blocks from the south end of the Doumer Bridge. Formerly a villa occupied by a high-ranking French colonialist, it featured a two-story grand house in the center of a walled area several hundred feet square. Within the walls the servant quarters and storage buildings had been converted to prison cells; they were nasty stone cubicles which had no ventilation, heat, or water.

We were placed in cells in which the barred windows had been bricked shut. Our confinement was dungeon-like. Our latrine was a two-gallon bucket that sat in the corner, often without a lid to curb the stench. Our only breath of fresh air came from the crack under the heavily chained and bolted door. We were rarely allowed outside the cell. For years we lived in one and two-man rooms. Our bed was a flat wooden platform on two wooden sawhorses. An eighth-inch-thick, roll-up rice mat was our mattress.

Each prisoner was divested of all clothing, watches and jewelry when captured. The captive was issued prison garb that identified him as a criminal. The clothing consisted of light cotton pajamas; black or maroon and gray striped. We had two pairs of shorts, two short-sleeved shirts, two long legged pairs of pants and two long-sleeved shirts. We were issued black rubber clogs made from tire treads. We were issued two cotton blankets, a mosquito net, a tin cup, a one-liter water container and a toothbrush with a small tube of toothpaste that was labeled "Good Taste-Much Bubble". These items were expected to last forever. Reluctantly our captors issued replacement toothbrushes and clogs about every year or two.

The camp cook was allowed very little budget to feed the fifty-seven men held at the Plantation. Therefore, she boiled huge pots of watery soup, twice daily, of the cheapest vegetable in the market place. When pumpkins were in season, we had a bowl of pumpkin soup twice per day. The cook had no obligations to provide variety or tastiness. We once counted 140 bowls of pumpkin soup in a row.

When the pumpkin season was over, cabbage was used, then green finger-size bananas, then an edible Morning Glory vine we called *sewer greens*. Since the guards preferred eating rice with every meal, we were fed crude bread made of wheat from Russia (complete with weevils). The tough bread was the size of a dinner roll and augmented the soup. Nutritionally, our meals were not far from being bread and water. Many men suffered from vitamin deficiencies that were irreversible when repatriated such as loss of bone density, spots in their vision etc.

To her credit, the cook attempted to flavor the soup with whatever she could find: generous quantities of salt, fat back (with hair still on it), small dog, and an occasional bit of monkey (one cellmate found a little hand in his soup.) With a sense of survival the POWs ate everything offered to them.

At The Plantations, Captain Larry Carrigan and I were in Showroom One; Corncrib Three; Longhouse 12, 9, 7 and 6; and finally Gun Shed One. The Gun Shed, so named for the old French cannon that sat in front of it, was both good and bad. It was good to be housed in the Gun Shed because we believed it was reserved for the prisoners that were least deserving of the *humane and lenient treatment*. It gave us status among our peers to be housed in the Gun Shed with the other three rooms of prisoners deemed to have *the bad attitude* by the North Vietnamese. Carrigan and I had been caught communicating with the other prisoners thirteen times the first year. Considering we communicated about one thousand times we reasoned that a 1.3% failure rate was acceptable.

The down side of being in the Gun Shed was that it had a flat, black roof that heated the cells to 135 degrees Fahrenheit every day of the summer months. Our room actually had a window in the end of the building with louvered shutters covering the bars rather than bricks. We could at least see downward at a steep angle and observe the bugs, ants, spiders, or ducks that happen to go by the six foot span between our cell and the camp latrine.

One day the camp commander acquired two potbellied pigs and penned them outside our window with a makeshift fence to span the six feet. Kitchen leftovers fattened the pigs for the future feast of the camp commander. Carrigan, an urban cowboy from Phoenix, had little experience with farm animals. They repulsed him. So I slept next to the end window, just eight or ten inches away from the smelly, grunting, snoring pigs that we called Heckle and Jeckle.

One afternoon Carrigan observed that Heckle ate all he wanted before allowing Jeckle to eat anything at all. Carrigan considered this grossly unfair and decide to set things right. The moment Heckle buried his snout into the slop up to his eyes, Carrigan splashed a cup of his valuable water ration on him. Heckle jumped in surprise. The second time Carrigan startled the beast, the pigs bolted through the flimsy retaining fence and raced across the courtyard.

"Now you've done it!" I said, "If we get a beating because of you frightening the camp commander's pigs, I am going to kick your fanny when the guards get through with us."

Predictably, the guards came racing across the courtyard to our room and began opening the bolts and chains. Glaring at Carrigan, I repeated, "Remember, I'm going to get you for this."

The guards opened our door and entered with wide eyes. "The camp commander's pigs have escaped! He will be angry with us. Do you know how to catch the pigs for us?"

"Sure," I said, "We'd be glad to help you with the pigs." Relieved that the guards believed that they were to blame, I volunteered our services. Actually, we welcomed every opportunity to get out of our own stinking little pen.

Thankfully, I had learned pig catching as a boy while visiting my cousin on his family farm in Arkansas. The technique requires hemming the pig in a corner, spreading your legs wide enough to allow the near-sighted pig to see the escape route between your legs. When the pig pass under you, catch his rear legs and lift them off the ground. Then step back and over as if getting out of a saddle. This rolls the pig onto his back and renders him helpless. However, the pig will squeal to high heaven as if he was being murdered.

Carrigan and I jogged after the pigs around the court yard, enjoying our outing for fifteen or twenty minutes. Finally, we hemmed one of the pigs in a corner. I approached the pig with my legs wide apart. He bolted for freedom. I caught his hind legs and rolled him onto his back. The guards applauded the effort. With a bit of coaxing, Carrigan cautiously seized one front leg and one back leg to assist me returning the pigs one by one upside down to the pen.

That affair turn out so well, we planned on working the "Spook the Pigs" deal again when we wanted to get a breath of fresh air outside of our cell. Regrettably, the pigs were butchered and served to the camp commander and staff shortly thereafter. However, I was relieved not to hear their snoring the following months.

"POWs Never Have A Nice Day" read a sad-faced lapel button worn by those back home who attempted to bring national attention to the plight of military detainees in Vietnam in the late 60s. It was true. The hardships were physical and psychological. Poor nutrition and medical care were life threatening. Long-term duress was a deep and dangerous problem as well. To my knowledge four men in the prison camps succumbed to deep depression which lead to insanity and death. There was little any of us could do for them.

The men who were able to accommodate to prison life and the subhuman status accorded the American POWs were amazingly resilient warriors. Although our training in service survival schools had informed us of what conditions were likely to be, living through them was another matter! It was a struggle on a daily basis in the prison camps: a struggle to survive the physical and medical hazards, a struggle to resist the enemy's constant efforts to propagandize the captives to benefit their worldwide image, and a struggle to cope with the tragedy of separation from the families who agonized for us each instant of our confinement.

The POW's day began at daylight with a guard pounding on a length of iron railroad rail suspended from a tree branch. The clanging signaled the beginning of their workday and our challenge to struggle through yet another day of existence.

The turnkey guard quickly opened each cell one by one in order to have us set our two-gallon bucket of urine and waste outside the cell door. He then relocked the door. A work crew of POWs collected the buckets, dumped them in to the camp reservoir (they saved it for fertilizer), rinsed and returned them to the cell doors. The turnkey repeated the opening and relocking procedure to put the buckets back within the cells.

The bucket routine gave us opportunity to exchange notes in the bucket lids. Note exchanges are really not a very good idea because, if discovered, both the writer and the receiver were undeniably guilty of breaking the camp regulations. This often led to severe punishment. Further, the information in the note was compromised.

The camp commander, under the policy of Ho Chi Minh, had issued and elaborate set of camp regulations, among them was:

"The criminal must maintain silence in the detention rooms and not make any loud noises which can be heard outside. All schemes and attempts to gain information and achieve communication with the criminals living next door by intentionally talking loudly, tapping on walls or other means will be strictly punished [tortured.]"

Carrigan and I, having the end room of the Gun Shed had a view of the two POWs emptying the buckets. The two men selected for the odious task to empty and rinse the buckets realized we were watching.

Lieutenant James Shively was shot down in an F-105 over North Vietnam on May 5, 1967 and Lieutenant Commander Joe Crecca was shot down in his F-4 early on in November of 1966. The two men took turns empting and rinsing the buckets while the other stood adjacent to the guard. The guard always stood far enough away to avoid the smell of the dumping.

The POW positioned himself shoulder to shoulder between the guard and our window. With the hand nearest our window, he was able to finger the Tap Code without being detected. Bravely these two sent us news from around the camp each morning for more than a year. We were made aware of who had been to *Quiz* (interrogation) and what sort of propaganda the captor was seeking now as well as other camp news and gossip.

Carrigan loved receiving the morning news. It was like reading the sports page. He pressed his face to the louvered and barred window each day to receive the finger-coded news. I spent these moments with my bottom up and head to the floor peeping under the crack of our door to assure that the communicating pair was clear of other guards that might be watching. Should another guard be detected, a throat clearing or pretend sneeze would serve as a warning to stop communicating.

Then one day, our clever communication link had a crisis. Apparently the camp commander had challenged the guards to grow productive plants in the courtyard, perhaps as a competition. Our turnkey planted a climbing squash plant directly in the line-of sight of our communication link. The tropical sun and abundant fertilizer (our own waste products) caused the plant to flourish, producing huge leaves which blocked our view. This was a challenge to Carrigan's communication skills.

At his next opportunity (which was a couple of agonizing weeks without the morning sports page), Carrigan furtively approached the plant and snapped off the base at the ground level. He quickly pushed the stem into the earth and departed the area. It was our thought that in a day or two the plant would wilt and die. It would be unlikely that we would be associated with the plant's demise. The "day or two" assumption was wrong. Within ten minutes the tropical sun caused the leaves to wilt and the plant to enter its death throes.

The turnkey noticed his plant immediately. He reported to the camp commander who, with most of his staff, rushed to the scene. In a close inspection they found the snapped-off stem. Carrigan and I watched the grim faces of our captors and wondered what horrible fate was to befall us for our part in the death of the plant.

The camp commander stood erect with jutted chin and made an authoritative speech. Although Carrigan and I spoke very little of the Vietnamese language, we surmised the gist of the declaration. The camp commander accused one of the other competing guards not yet identified for this heartless deed since the turnkey's plant had a commanding lead. Therefore, the turnkey was declared the winner of the competition. A round of applause and handshakes followed. The proud turnkey returned to his duties. Carrigan and I breathed a sigh of relief. Close calls and small triumphs like this kept us alive and optimistic. You can't buy thrills like that.

One incident occurred while Larry and I were in the Gun Shed that could have cost us a great deal of pain. It occurred one hot night in August. The temperature in the cell was extremely high. There was no ventilation to allow the heat to escape during the night. Therefore, Carrigan and I removed all our clothing after we tucked ourselves under the mosquito net. Our bodies were wet with sweat from the summer sun's warming the black, flat top of the building. We fanned with our wicker fan until fatigue overtook us and slumber was possible.

One night we heard the walk-around night guard kicking the door.

Carrigan said, "Somebody is at the door."

I responded, "Tell him I am in the shower."

Carrigan responded, "No. You are the senior officer here. You have to deal with him."

Reluctantly, I crawled out from under the protection of the mosquito net and was immediately attacked by a hundred pests. As I approached the door, I saw the guard's nose and eyes peering through the tiny little inspection door. His wide-eyed fix on my nakedness caused me to place my hand over my genitals in modesty. He squawked and slammed the little slide to shut the inspection door.

Carrigan asked, "What did he want?"

I commented, "I guess he just wanted a full shot. He took off."

I crawled back under my mosquito net and set about killing the pests that were tapped into my blood supply.

Then we heard the chatter of several Vietnamese headed our way. Keys rattled and the heavy wooden cross bar was removed. The door swung open wide.

Our daytime turnkey who spoke fair English entered and barked, "Getup! Put on long!" meaning put on long PJ's.

This was the required attire when we were in the presence of an NVN Officer. We dressed and two riflemen came into the cell and backed us up to wall. A short NVN Officer slowly entered with his hands clasp behind his back. (Hollywood could not have scripted this scene better.)

He asked, "Who told you to sleep *no clothes on?*"

I replied, "It is not against our custom. Even if I were sleeping with my wife and it was this hot we would sleep *no clothes on.*"

He gave a look of disgust and snapped, "That is a dirty way to live!"

In the orient men do not customarily show nudity to each other. They wear bikini underwear when in a common shower.

The Officer pointed an accusing finger at me and barked, "You! You have made an obscene sign to this man."

He gestured toward a seething mad guard who stared directly at me in pure hatred.

"You must apologize to him for your bad behavior!"

I said, "I don't know any obscene signs in Vietnamese; tell him I'm sorry to upset him."

With a curt nod he turned and made about a three page apology on my behalf to the night guard. Gradually, he cooled down and left as did the armed guards and officer. The daytime turnkey remained behind to explain to us why we had had the problem.

135

He explained, "In Vietnam the worst sign one man can show another man is to place his hand over his genitals. No do again"

Camp Hope (Son Tay)

On December the sixth of 1969, I was transferred along with a lot of the other prisoners, including my roommate Larry Carrigan, to a camp north of Hanoi, which was named by the POWs as *Camp Hope*. It was set out in the middle of a plain. There was a little river that ran by the back edge of it which sometimes flooded. It had an eight foot wall around it with broken glass and barbed wire on the top edge. Guard towers were located on the corners so that everybody could be seen. Outside of the walls of the camp were the barracks, the meeting places, and the gardens of the guard compliment. Inside were three cellblocks that we named *Opium Den, Beerhall,* and *Cathouse*.

The structures within the camp were all masonry. Interesting enough they did have tile roofs, and I suppose that could be considered a design fault for a prison. We could have gone straight up through our ceiling, which was fairly flimsy, taken off tiles and gotten out. Maybe we could possibly have gone over the wall unnoticed in a rainstorm. But, the probability of an American POW getting anywhere after he got out was low because we were in the middle of an Asian country and we're not hard to recognize as being the enemy. So, we never attempted an escape from Camp Hope. The facility wasn't bad except the water source was really poor. Perhaps that was the reason Camp Hope was abandoned by the North Vietnamese and moved over to another camp called *Camp Faith*.

Camp Hope, which held over sixty people, was located twenty-five miles north of Hanoi. When we arrived there we found twelve prisoners in Camp Hope who were shortly transferred back into the prison camp in Hanoi. We had no idea why the North

Vietnamese shuffled prisoners around like that. We never got an idea for any of those reasons; but what it did serve was that we brought all the names we had in our corporate memory out there to them and took theirs into our lists, which was a great help. They had received no news from the outside world for a whole year. In the first year that Camp Hope was open there was harsh, harsh treatment at the camp. During that year, Ho Chi Minh was still alive then; when I arrived there Ho Chi Minh was dead and there was no harsh treatment. The North Vietnamese admonished us not to tap on the walls or do anything like pass notes around, which we were going to do anyway.

The first day I was at Camp Hope they told us, "This is a working camp. And, you will have to help us break up bricks for a foundation for the new quiz room."

The guards handed us a steel pipe, a section about eighteen inches long, and instructed us to bust up old bricks. A steel pipe in the hands of a POW was tantamount to a telegraph key. We simply accepted the task requested of us and tapped *a shave and a haircut*. We heard people coughing all over the camp in response.

I said, "We're online, guys."

We began to tell them we were twelve guys from the Plantation, the Plantation has 57 guys, our SRO is Ted Guy, and on and on. With the preliminaries out of the way we then got to the news of the day.

I think we told them Neil Armstrong had walked on the Moon. And that, a turbine car had led the Indianapolis brickyard race for a 198 laps before a small gear had failed--otherwise it would have won the race easily. We shared little things like that. We knew they'd like to know who had won the NFL championship. All this seemingly mundane news was morale boosting information the guys always asked of a new shoot down. Nobody that I know of received a beating or even isolation at Camp Hope that last year.

The rooms in Camp Hope usually had multiple people in them. Larry and I had been living together for two-and-a-half years before as a twosome. Arriving at Son Tay they put another guy in with us, Capt. Irby David Terrell, who was a navigator on a B-66 shot down by a MiG-21 northwest of Thanh Hoa near the Laotian border.

We had easy communication with the *Beerhall*. But, we were never turned outside to visit with anybody. When we were outside for any work chore we were just one room at a time. We noticed some of the rooms at the *Beerhall* had a dozen people in them. So, it was not bad. Our confinement at Camp Hope wasn't really a difficult task for the year I was there. However, I understand the previous year was pretty horrible. But as indicated earlier, Ho Chi Minh was gone during my first year living in the camp, and it was generally *live and let live* as far as our treatment was concerned.

There was a continual effort to give us schooling—indoctrination if you please. The North Vietnamese didn't call it a *quiz* as we termed it or even an interrogation. The North Vietnamese thought of it more as *the POWs need to know the North Vietnamese perspective of the war.* They were couched in a category of passive indoctrination.

Their officers implied, "We are not attempting to brainwash you into thinking our systems are better. We realize you are too steeped in Imperialism and you're not going to become a communist. But you're going to have to listen to our perspective of the world while you are here."

And, it seemed to be a legitimate thing for them to do--to attempt to convince us regarding our barbarous bombing of the South, tearing up all their airfields, and destroying their bridges and railroad yards.

There was no brutality in this schooling; and it wasn't a heavy indoctrination program. Once a month I'd see some designated indoctrination official in the camp and they'd want to give me some kind of information about their country. And when I refused to write any written responses they just shrugged and went on their way. They entered in their book, "Baker's been told about this subject." So, I think the camp commander did have the responsibility of continuing this education of the prisoners and checking off all these various subjects, like "Woman's role in the Peoples Republic" and the "Atrocities of sowing insects on their rice fields," or something like that. That type of practice prevailed throughout the remainder of my stay in Camp Hope.

The Raid on Son Tay (Camp Hope)

An interesting thing about Camp Hope is that when we were finally moved out of the camp, the North Vietnamese did not repopulate it with other prisoners. The guards and camp commanders stayed there. They just didn't keep prisoners there for the time being. And, that cost them their lives. The Air Force air surveillance of these outlying camps was constantly and continually taking pictures of the camps. As far as Air Force Intelligence could tell Camp Hope was still occupied. On an aerial photograph their underwear looks like our underwear hanging on the close lines. In addition there were a host of other things from which the intelligence specialist take their clues, which said we were still occupying the camp.

When it came time for US forces to execute the rescue attempt at Son Tay (Camp Hope), even though they'd been planning it for a year, they were unaware we had packed up in the still of night and left. The enemy were the only ones left at the camp. When the raiders assaulted the camp they eliminated certain basic targets, all of the guards, and anyone else around it. The raiders simply shot everything up that was outside of that camp and crashed a helicopter into the camp. They then assaulted the gates and entrances with bolt cutters and cut all the locks off and discovered there were no prisoners.

However, they found about a dozen guys, Vietnamese guards, sleeping in the Beerhall. Those guards lost their lives as they came spilling out of the Beerhall. The Son Tay raiders just cut them up and none of those survived. As far as I know there was one survivor outside of that camp. Along the road there were some civilian huts and there was one lady who got under her bed and didn't race to the country side like everybody else did. When they saw the raid begin they left because they were so close to it. Years later that particular lady was interviewed and she told about the raid from the Vietnamese perspective.

Camp Faith

We were moved from Camp Hope to Camp Faith on July 6, 1970. Camp Faith was actually a barracks set up for the Vietnamese or at least that is how it seemed. But, it worked just fine for a prison camp, because like any army post it had a wall around it. It was divided into four sections, as I recall. It was of masonry construction and the rooms were large. We put all the O-5s and O-4s, lieutenant colonels and majors, in one room and then we put the captains and lieutenants in another room, which was all right. In the daytime we were all out in the common courtyard and interacted. It was amazing. That was the first time we ever had any interaction with that many people. We could see over the wall and there was another set of barracks that was unoccupied. It could have been an army post at one time.

It was at this camp that I was able to greet Captain Richard "Gene" Smith. We hugged and slapped backs like long lost brothers. Gene has a marvelous sense of humor. He immediately blamed his shoot down on me for not giving him his lesson on *How Not to Get Shot Down.*

Sharing the prison ordeal with guys like Gene Smith, Larry Carrigan, Dave Terrell, Jon Reynolds, Smitty Harris, Leon Ellis and countless others made the miserable existence bearable if not fun at times.

The guards who attended us there were from downtown, Hanoi. The Camp Hope guards stayed in Son Tay for reasons unknown to me.

We'd been around these camps enough that we got to know by sight a lot of the guards. We never befriended them, because we were told not to do that. It was our policy not to befriend the guard because he may ask some things of you that you cannot provide. And he doesn't really have much intelligence to gain which you could use. He's a low-ranking soldier. Our policy in the camp was don't befriend them and get into a casual conversation unless it is forced upon you. We abided by that rule.

We knew most of these guys. And we knew which ones used to be harsh and tyrannical, but that was Ho Chi Minh's policy. By the time I got to Camp Faith they were improving in their personal contempt of Americans. I mean they knew their job. We never got into any conflict with anybody at that particular camp. That was a short term camp.

The treatment at Camp Faith was even better than that at Camp Hope. I don't recall ever having a quiz, interview, or brainwashing session while we were there. It was just captivity. Occasionally an interrogator would come in and walk through and talk to people. I think this guy was just a reader, a censor. We found out fairly early that if you get a friendly English speaking officer walking through your camp he's just trying to check out some things he doesn't understand in some letter he's going to get you to talk about.

One prisoner, who had a terrible case of hemorrhoids, requested in a letter for his mother to send him some suppositories. However, he did it in such a manner as to not mention it directly but rather in a subtle written code. He asked his mother to send him some of his favorite candy,   *Roids*. He hoped she would understand his subtle reference and send him some Preparation-H suppositories. The censor guy apparently intercepted the letter and was confused about the terms. He happened to encounter me on an occasion when I was outside my room.

The censure guy wandered up to me casually and remarked, "Hey, Baker, How are you today? Do you like candy?"

"Sure, I like candy," I answered.

He asked, "Do you ever eat *Roids*?"

I thought, *damn, this is the censor talking,*

I replied, "Oh, yeah, I love them. They come in this little tin foil wrapper. They are kind of shaped like a bullet. They don't taste particularly good, but some people really like them." I then asked, "Have you got any?"

He answered abruptly, "No, I don't have any." Then he just sort of walked off.

I looked up that particular POW who wrote the letter and said, "You're the luckiest guy in the world. The censor got to talk to somebody who knew what a *Roid* was."

Months later the POW received a letter from his mother who said. "Say again what kind of candy you want." Mom didn't understand *Roids* either.

We only stayed at Camp Faith for six months. The very morning after the Son Tay (Camp Hope) nighttime raid, we were moved from Camp Faith. Six-by-six trucks drove into the camp, the North Vietnamese loaded us into the trucks, and away we went to downtown Hanoi. They envisioned the Son Tay raid might be just the first of many raids of the outlying POW camps. Our new home was the part of Hoa Lo prison, the Hanoi Hilton, which we called Camp Unity.

Camp Unity (Hoa Lo Prison, Hanoi Hilton)

In November of 1970 I made my second visit to the Hanoi Hilton. My first visit had been during my initial interrogation where I spent my first twenty days at *New Guy Village*. This move back to the Hanoi Hilton would place me in a forty-man room in what we knew as Camp Unity.

The Hanoi Hilton was actually a compound comprised of a series of structures. Each area was known by its own special name. *New Guy Village* was where the newly captured flyers were taken in the very first days of their captivity. As detailed earlier in this account, those first days were characteristic of extreme pain and displeasure, where torture was the norm. After the North Vietnamese were satisfied they had expended all the information and/or propaganda which could be squeezed from a man, he was moved to other accommodations. I had been moved from New Guy Village to the Plantation and had made my rounds through the other camps to eventually turn up again at Camp Unity, a section of the Hanoi Hilton.

The structure was built by the French in 1890 as a prison to hold Vietnamese political prisoners. Vietnam was at that time a subject of the French in French Indochina. Prisoners held there were typically those agitating for independence. At its height it held more than 2,000 prisoners, although it was designed for around 600.

It is located in the center of Hanoi and as such its name, Maison Central (Central House,) is appropriate. After the French were defeated at Dien Bien Phu and vacated Vietnam in 1954, the Vietnamese renamed the prison Hoa Lo, which literally means *fiery furnace* or *Hell's hole*. The tortuous and inhumane treatments practiced by the French were enhanced and perfected by the North

Vietnamese within the walls of this prison. The American prisoners of war bitterly and sarcastically renamed it the *Hanoi Hilton.*

There is some discussion as to who, when, and how it received this nickname. However, one story attributes it to Lieutenant Commander Bob Shumaker, an F-8D pilot shot down on February 11, 1965. The story recognizes Shumaker as the first to write it down when carving "Welcome to the Hanoi Hilton" on the handle of a pail to greet the arrival of Lieutenant Robert Peel who was shot down on May 31, 1965. Regardless of the origin of the nickname, it has come to symbolize the cruelty of the North Vietnamese to American POWs and the fortitude and bravery exhibited by those same POWs.

We were contained in a large cell that had a fifty-man common bed made of concrete in the middle of the room, which was over seventy feet in length. There were great advantages to being confined in the big forty-man room of Camp Unity. The activities revitalized the POWs who had suffered years and years being confined in one or two-man rooms. However, the larger room did have its hazards. The emboldened group began to devise elaborate schemes to gain advantage over the captor in one manner or the other.

Emergency escape plans were developed in case of sudden invasion by US forces or sudden floods from a dam break in the Red River. Essential to these plans were good communications on the weather and the status of the war efforts in North Vietnam. To this end, the members of Room Three asked me to design and fabricate a radio to listen to Hanoi Hanna, a propaganda program aimed at American GIs in South Vietnam.

I organized a small cadre to scavenge the needed parts, fabricate the tiny radio, and secure the apparatus during and after the development process. The process was well underway in the fall of 1971.

We created a tiny speaker using the cone of the top of a toothpaste tube. With masticated bread we glued stiff brown paper, which was provided by our captors as toilet paper, to the face of the cone. Inside the tube opening we inserted a coil made from fine wire filched from the propaganda squawk box found in every room in the camp. A small nail ramrod extended from the paper diaphragm through the coil to a small, round magnet someone had stolen from the Camp Commander's chess set. The small magnet pulled the nail rod aft and any small current through the coil pulled the nail forward.

Since the Hanoi radio antenna was only a few blocks away, a strong, induced radio signal existed in the seventy-foot steel wire that extended from one end of the room to the other. This wire was to suspend one end of our mosquito nets over the forty-man concrete bed that occupied the center of the room. Capturing the signal could be accomplished with a tuned resonance trap consisting of a coil similar to the speaker coil and a capacitor made of parallel razorblade chips. Another small nail was used to slip in and out of the coil of the trap to tune the trap's resonance to the frequency of Hanoi Hanna's carrier wave. Thus the audio signal of Hanna's voice could be found on one end of the trap. This signal went to the speaker coil and powered the oscillations of the tiny paper diaphragm. We could have listened nightly to glean information from Hanna's broadcasts.

Our project security man placed the parts of the partially completed radio in a small vial. To the vial he tied a black thread and suspended the jar in the brown sludge within the bombsight latrine vat. We were confident that the project was secure. However, the Vietnamese had seen this gambit before. On a routine shakedown inspection, the jar of electronics was discovered.

Invariably, in a large room there is at least one POW that has been brutalized so badly in the past that he can be intimidated again for information about who might have been behind this project. Obviously, the Vietnamese quickly learned of my involvement and leadership in the project. As the shakedown inspection came to the end, the Room Three inmates were patted down one-by-one and returned to the room. I noticed that I was slowly being isolated from my cellmates. When all of my cellmates were tucked into confinement, six guards circled me and roughly placed my hands behind my back in manacles. They shoved me across camp into Heartbreak Hotel, a block of a dozen cells reserved for the blackest of the *black criminals*.

"Now you must confess your crimes and ask for the Camp Commander's forgiveness or you will receive severe punishment," the lead guard shouted at me when he slammed shut the steel door and latched the heavy bolt.

I had no intention of confessing to anything until I found out which project of mine they discovered. In my bedroll. I had a very nice bamboo ink pen I had made for writing in microprint the many French verbs we were beginning to accumulate in our studies. I did not wish to lose that.

We had learned to make ink. A POW knowledgeable in chemistry tapped the method to us. The starch water obtained from squeezing wet cooked rice through a rag is a hydrocarbon that converts to carbon ink when mixed with a little bit of iodine. I had asked the guard for iodine for my foot fungus (we all had it.) The guard issued me a pea size cotton ball soaked in iodine and watched as I treated my fungus. The leftover cotton ball had plenty of iodine to make a thimble full of ink.

The next morning I was marched from Heartbreak to the camp commander. He was sullen and smoldering. He accused me of communicating with the CIA.

He demanded, "You must write down every conversation you have had with the CIA."

At the very least, he accused me of making a homing device for the B-52s. Now that I knew what project they had discovered, I began to talk my way out of trouble. I told him it was true that I was making a radio receiver but it was not true that it was a transmitter. It was just a little radio to listen to the Hanoi Radio for news of the war. Naturally, we are all wondering how the war is going. For some reason the camp squawk box had ceased broadcasting anything. I told him we were all curious, and I meant no harm. Simply put, I was just trying to help keep the POWs calm and their morale high since the camp radio seemed to be broken.

The camp commander growled and insisted the camp radio did work and he alone had the authority to say when we could hear news of the war. Now, I must suffer for my crimes and must write my confession. There can be no forgiveness unless I confess my *black crimes* and ask to be returned to the *humane and lenient treatment* with my cellmates.

From Heartbreak Hotel I was taken to the nastiest, darkest isolation cell that I knew of in the whole prison. The cell seemed to be stereotypical of a bad Friday Night horror movie. It was the bottom of a silo-like structure built at the corner of the prison walls separating the large rooms that we had numbered Room Two and Room Three. At the top of the silo was a parapet with stone slots resembling a castle. From there the guard could see the length of each wall, watching for escapees. In the center of his round walkway was a grate that allowed him to peer thirty feet below to the poor souls confined there.

The French built this dungeon to confine Vietnamese prisoners during the colonial years prior to 1954. This particular cell could hold seven tightly packed Vietnamese prisoners. At the bottom of the silo there was an inclined concrete bed with a curb at the foot of the bed. The curb had fourteen semicircular cutouts for prisoner ankles. A steel bar bolted down all seven prisoners' ankles.

In the colonial days the prisoners remained in the ankle stocks day after day. At the foot of the concrete bed was a sewage ditch that emptied to the street outside. The prisoners, unable to move, soiled themselves. They were occasionally washed down with a deluge of water from the grate high overhead. Through that same grate entered the only light to the cell.

Fortunately, the steel bar for locking down the prisoner ankles was rusted away. I was able to stride around my ten-by-ten bed and exercise daily.

Before slamming the steel door, the guard handed me an ink pen and three sheets of fine writing paper. This, I was informed, was to be used for my confession and request for forgiveness. What luck! I had need of a good supply of ink and lots of paper. A few days earlier, I had a deep discussion with another POW about the need for a logarithm table. The other POWs were beginning to query me about how much their wives could have saved in the 10% overseas savings plan by now. The task would be simpler to calculate if we had a log-table. My mathematical friend, an MIT graduate, had amused himself with the same problem a few years earlier and derived the infinite series that would compute the table one entry at a time. The computation would take days and a lot of meticulous calculations to develop a rudimentary three-place table. Happy Day! The enemy had presented to me pen, ink and paper for the work.

In the dim light of my silo cell, I rapidly made all the calculations possible with the ink and paper provided me. With the last of the watered down ink supply, I mico-printed the results and slipped the small rolled paper in the hem of my blanket. I had slightly more than half of the log-table completed.

The next day of my confinement, the guard demanded my completed confession. With my best sad face, I reported that despite my attempts, nothing came out right. Moreover, I had to use the fine paper for toilet paper since he had not left enough. Furious, he left and returned with a new supply of toilet paper, pen and ink, and fine confession paper.

I worked every daylight hour on my project. Completing the log table, I secured it in the blanket hem. I shredded all the notes and the toilet paper as well before dumping them once again in the toilet bucket. I calmly awaited the guard the next day. When he arrived I preempted his demand for my confession with a request to see the camp medic for some diarrhea medicine. He grumbled that he thought I was wasting the people's paper and left with the empty pen. Nobody made further demands for a confession and I had my log table.

This exciting bit of duping the captor consumed less than a week. I was likely to be down in this hole for the duration. What will I do with the rest of the time? Just then a burned out wooden matchstick fell through the overhead grill and lit at my feet. That must have been the source of charcoal the former occupant of this room used to start the drawing of a lady's face that I found on the wall. Beneath the half done portrait were the words "Indonesian Ali". Ali had, in his loneliness, started a portrait of his true love that he will perhaps never see again. I felt a kinship with Ali. I felt moved to finish his lady's portrait. It may take weeks or months, depending on how heavily the guards smoke. I had time to wait on my daily delivery of tiny charcoal sticks.

Two weeks later Ali's Love was complete. It was my finest charcoal work. Ms. Charlene Macke Pruitt, my high school art teacher would have approved.

However, the hours of the day would be long and boring unless I conjured up another mind-bending challenge. That challenge arrived through the iron door in the form of another POW, Commander Claude Douglas, who was the Senior Ranking Officer (SRO) of Room Three. The camp commander had decided Clower must share some of the punishment I was receiving because he allowed such *black crimes* to be committed in Room Three. Clower came and shared my rat-infested domicile for forty-five days. Doug was from Mississippi. He spoke a brand of Southern

English dialect that mystified the Vietnamese and was a constant source of confusion and amusement to me.

We sat about the business of gaining contact with Room Three. We concluded that tapping on the wall had to travel through several feet of stone from our silo cell to the latrine of Room Three. It could be done but not discretely. I had attempted contact on my own earlier. I had to pound on the wall with the knob on top of our porcelain cup lid. The clanging aroused the guard above who sent the turnkey to check on me. The turnkey found me leaning against the wall listening to hear if Room Three answered. He asked what I was doing. I told him I had a bad toothache and was cooling it with the cold stonewalls. Doug and I would have to be more careful.

With careful listening to the overhead guard we could determine when he was gone or dormant. When we could not hear the overhead guard walking around, I rapped the shave-and-a-haircut call up signal. Room Three responded and sent us greetings as well as the news of the day. Owing to the noisy clanging we had to make with the cup lid, we kept our daily reports brief.

Clower and I had forty-five days of reviewing each other's life story and military career. We shared our thoughts on the men of room Three and their morale. We rarely complained about the food or our plight. We were just two GIs doing our duty regardless of the environment and hardships. Oddly, we had a lot of laughs during his stay. Doug had learned not to take life too seriously, particularly if you could not do anything about it. I have always marveled at the American GI's ability to make jokes about their darkest hours.

Clower and I recalled a story tapped though the wall earlier in Room Three that was a wonderful example of the American GI's courage and ability to never feel sorry himself. It seems that two POWs in one of the outlying camps had a falling out with the turnkey guard. While removed from their room to the water trough for their weekly bath, the turnkey sneaked back to their room, and with his knife he dug out some of the mortar around one of the window bars. Then he rushed to the commander of that camp and reported that the two POWs were trying to escape; fingering one of the POWs as the most likely offender.

The commander had the offender taken out of the room for punishment. The torture method was to place a steel bar across the back, place U-bolts over the biceps, tighten them until it was practically steel against bone. The POW remained in this state until dark.

The POW was returned to his cell and roommate near lifeless and with severely swollen arms. As he entered his cell his roommate exclaimed,

"You look like hell"

The POW replied "Don't feel sorry for me. You are the one that has to help me take a whiz for the next six weeks."

We became accommodated to the frequent visits of the ten-inch wharf rats whose territorial rights predated ours by a hundred years. We chased them away during our waking hours and tolerated them during our slumber.

Doug and I held Sunday services, as was the custom though out the American POW camps from day one. Somebody in the camp would signal the rest of the camp with a loud fake sneeze mid-morning Sundays. In that way, each cell entered worship services at the same time. It was during this time I allowed myself to think about my wife and children as well as other loved ones. I limited myself to just one hour per week of this reflection since the time was very emotional. I did not want the enemy to witness my emotion.

Doug was a great diversion for me during his stay. He never lost his appetite regardless of the duress we were under or the quality of the swill. He could suck down gut soup as if it was a southern delicacy. To him, life was never dull or boring; tomorrow things would be better. It occurred to me that his attitude was the secret to being a durable POW. One must have indomitable optimism, faith and a good sense of humor.

Strangely, the day came when the little steel door opened and Doug was ordered to return to the big room Three. I was to continue to suffer for my *black crimes*, the guard said.

Now that Doug was back in room Three, I checked in daily at an agreed upon time and stayed abreast of all the camp gossip. In between time, I concentrated on getting some work done on my chosen mental projects. I had started a three-volume cowboy novel with a hero that looked a great deal like me with a running mate named Larry Carrigan (my cellmate for over three years). I needed to finish the trilogy. I wanted to have it ready in a few months in case I should return to the big room. For entertainment we took turns in the big room telling stories or movies. I was sure they would like a Western.

Another mental project that occupied nearly a week was the tenth root of ten. It occurred to me that some monk in a monastery, whiling away time, had probably devised the way we do square roots long hand. Although I was taught in high school how to do square roots long hand, nobody ever explained why it was done that way. I felt challenged to unravel that mystery. Surely the intensive math training that I had received in the Air Force Institute of Technology at Wright-Paterson Air Force Base had provided me with at least as many skills as the lonely monk in the monastery.

After some thought, I discovered the underlying reasons for the technique and applied them to doing a cube root; that is, calculating what number multiplied times itself three times would equal the object number. Doing cube roots was complex. I had to resort to makeshift charcoal pencils by using the tiny matchsticks dropped daily by the overhead guard through the grate in order to keep track of the many terms involved.

The forth root of any number was easier. One has only to do the square root twice to calculate the forth root. The fifth root of any number must be done the hard way again. It required dividing the digits into groups of five etc., like the square root method only vastly more complex. However, having calculated it, one needs only to take the square root of the fifth root to arrive at the tenth root. Incidentally, the tenth root of ten turned out to be 1.2589, a larger number than I expected. This number might prove useful to me later if I decide to create a log-table to the base ten. Satisfied that I was now a root master, I went on to other mental projects.

I had in mind composing a monolog presentation styled after Bill Cosby's "Noah." In that skit God calls on Noah to build an ark. Noah can't believe it's really Him, and complains bitterly about using cubits to measure, and having to clean up behind all of those animals--until it starts to rain, that is. My skit was about Joshua fighting the battle of Jericho (See Appendix B.)

I launched into the exercise of mental writing. It occupied countless hours. The days and weeks flew by. When I started to develop the comic dialog for "Joshua" I found myself laughing out loud at some of my own gags. My high school drama teacher, Ms. Wanda McCormick McAnnaly, would have enjoyed it. The overhead guard noticed my laughing and called down to the walk-around guard that something was wrong with me. The turnkey was summoned to open up the dungeon and have look. They found me smiling, setting cross-legged in the middle of my concrete bed enjoying my stay at the Hanoi Hilton, Room Two-and-a-Half.

I was returned to the big room after three months without explanation and without a long winded, threatening speech from the camp commander. It was as if the camp commander thought I had learned my lesson and served my time.

Upon reentering the big room with the other prisoners, Doug Clower called the room to attention and ordered the men to present the hand salute. I returned the salute and reported "Major Elmo C. Baker returning for duty, Sir."

Dogpatch (Cao Bang)

In early 1972, the North Vietnamese military relocated approximately 200 prisoners to a camp known as Dogpatch. It was located near Cao Bang within the sight of the Chinese border, It is believed the move was spurred by concerns the American Special Forces would attempt another rescue of prisoners, which if successful would greatly reduce the communist bargaining chips at the Peace Talks as well as cause a loss of face and incur devastating humiliation. The communist leaders considered it a significant deterrent to move great numbers of prisoners of war to a site within twenty miles of the Chinese border, believing that location would also discourage any US operations since there was a restricted 20-mile *No Fly* zone buffering North Vietnam's border with China. US Flyers were to refrain from entering that zone. The enemy was quick to take advantage of that restraint by locating a camp within the buffer.

I have no idea how they chose me to be in that group. It looked like an arbitrary slicing of the group in half. And 200 of us went up to the north in 6x6 trucks. We wore leg manacles and were under guard. It took a 30 hour trip to get up there because the roads were all bombed out, and it was like driving over a plowed field.

The North Vietnamese were afraid this convoy of POWs might be attacked, although we never had any strafing attacks in the North. The Air Force were not permitted strafe. The Navy may get away with it but we, the Air Force, were never allowed to strafe. All actions had to come from the Pentagon, rather the White House. So, we couldn't jump on targets of opportunity at all. But the Vietnamese didn't know that for sure; so, they traveled at night. And, it just beat us to pieces.

We were not allowed to get out of the truck to relieve ourselves or stretch our legs for the entire trip. They placed a bucket in each truck and passed it around among the POWs if they had to urinate. Everybody thought they had to urinate because their kidneys were taking such a bashing. Poor guys would just strain over the bucket until the next guy would yank it away from him saying, "Give it to me! I can do it. You can't do it." Rarely could we do it. We were dehydrated anyway and we really didn't need to urinate but it felt like we did. It's amazing that we could not pass water when the urge was so demanding.

When we finally arrived at Dogpatch we were really beaten up. We moved into the facilities in the dark of night. We had to occupy a camp that had been left to the jungle two years earlier. It was overrun with plant growth. It was a hassle to put that camp together and make it livable.

The structures at Dogpatch were all stucco and we were placed in rooms of about twenty people. You could count the rooms around the structure and there were about ten of those. So, it figures there were about 200 people in that camp. And I happened to be senior ranking officer in one of rooms. We called that room Shark, which was my call sign when I was shot down.

There we experienced a slight improvement in our condition. They actually let two of these twenty man rooms out for a walk-around in the camp to exercise their legs and interact with the other rooms at the same time. We had the names of men we had committed to memory; some of them I'd never seen the entire time of my captivity. This gave us the opportunity to get a visual ID and to shake hands with somebody we knew was there but had never seen.

Unfortunately, we had absolutely nothing to do. They still never let us get out and, for example, make a garden. They didn't have the kind of manpower to watch us. They could not risk that sort of freedom. But, they did add some protein to our diet. The camp commander probably didn't get much of an increase in budget even though he was required to improve our diet. One day they walked a limping, aged, old water buffalo into camp, slaughtered him, and we all received a little two ounce chunk of buffalo meat in our soup for a while. It's just amazing what that does to your body, when you've been hungry for protein for a long time.

Then came powdered fish from Denmark. It was so odiferous you couldn't believe it. Brown powdered fish salt-cured to just dust. That's what they do with trash fish; they salt-cure it until it's dehydrated entirely. It's awful. But, we were being served a lot of rice at that particular camp. So far you haven't heard me mention rice at all. Rarely did we ever see rice. Usually on Sunday when the cook didn't want to cook for two meals she'd cook a big batch of rice and feed us some of that. At Cao Bang camp, Dogpatch, we had rice at every meal. They put cracked corn in the rice to extend the amount. That was actually better than just plain straight rice.

In addition, they let us have salt. It was coarse salt like you and I put on our doorstep when it has ice on it. However, that was too much salt and your system couldn't take it. I mean you'd get an overdose of salt. What we did was crush it with our metal cups. We would put it in a pan and crush it into powder. We let the camp commander know that he was going to hear some banging noise over here because we've got to crush up this salt. He said, "I know. It's okay."

There was no more interrogation. If you had something to say to the camp commander you could call for an audience with him; and I did that one time because we were all getting dysentery since we couldn't keep our dishes clean. They wanted us to wash our own dishes but we didn't have hot water or soap. I did get a chance to talk to the camp commander in French. He liked to speak French and I knew enough of it from the classes we took at Camp

Unity. I learned to speak conversational French for survival reasons. The effort paid off. The Camp Commander heard my plea and agreed to allow us to heat dish water as well as provided a small measure of soap.

But, that little bit of protein in our food was a great help. In that final year we all put back on ten pounds of the fifty or so we had lost. The gastronomic prognosticators (GPs) had been right. This small group of POWs had for years maintained that the end of the hostilities and prisoner exchange would be signaled by a sharp increase of fruit in our rations. Our captors understood the need for fruit to avoid diseases such as beriberi. However, they saw no need to dole out fruit but once a month. Even then it was the cheapest the cook could buy at the market place.

Therefore, we were provided fruit such as green, unripened oranges and stunted pineapples no bigger than a baseball. The GPs forecast the end of our ordeal when we began to receive daily properly ripen fruit. And so it was, the week before we started our return trip to Hanoi we received fruit daily. You got to hand it to the GPs. They saw it coming.

The North Vietnamese saw the end coming. And, they mentioned that to us earlier. They said when we go back to Hanoi it will probably be over. And it was. In December of 1972 Nixon started the bombing. That brought them to the table. It caused them to agree to a cease fire and a prisoner exchange, and also to promise not to invade the South, which they did anyway.

The treatment was pretty decent at Dogpatch. We even saw one or two movies. This was kind of a thing with the Vietnamese. In all camps, their camps and our camps, they'd send around a propaganda team. They would show you how they were winning great and glorious battles. They were like RKO Newsreels--only the Vietnamese were always winning. They featured 14 year-old girls capturing shoot down pilots and things like that.

Our camp commander brought in a movie that was a Russian film with color. I had seen movies before in the Plantation, but they were of the RKO Newsreel type, and straight out North Vietnamese propaganda, which was for the North Vietnamese people, saying, "We are winning great and glorious battles down here overwhelming the Imperialist tiger." I guess I saw a half dozen of those while I was hanging around in the southern part of North Vietnam in those camps. The one or two movies we saw there at Dogpatch were not of the propaganda black and whites. The color entertainment was a wild switch, because the Vietnamese hardly did anything that was for our entertainment or pleasure. We had no rights for that and for that last year they apparently changed their mind.

The Plantation – Release Staging

They moved us back to the Plantation for our final move. . This was the staging place to make us a *go home* set of clothes. I was there for only a couple of months. But, the trip down from Dogpatch was entirely different than the trip up.

We were not in manacles. We were the same number of people in the six-by-six and we had two guards in there. They were sitting in the back. They had the canvas down on each side for they didn't want the populace to know there were Americans in these six-by-sixes. It was for our own safety. They stopped regularly once every hour-and-a-half out in the countryside. We would all get out and go to the bathroom and we would have an energy bar. It looked like a regular G.I. nourishment bar. They kept us watered.

They did it traveling in both day and night. It didn't take near as much time to get down. It took us 30 hours to get up to Dogpatch and I think we got down to Camp Plantation in Hanoi in 12 hrs.

A personal anecdote: we were crossing a pontoon bridge at the Bac Giang Bridge--It was the same bridge I had destroyed when

I got shot down and found out later they decided not to rebuild it anymore. They just stayed with a pontoon bridge. They placed pontoons across it during the night and then they would simply swing the pontoons against the shoreline during the daytime, putting it back out at night.

As we were crossing that pontoon bridge one of the guys nudged the guard and said, "Do you know where the bridge went?" Then he motioned to me and said, "Mo."

The guard responded dryly, "We know."

They knew that about me--that I was the one who made splinters out of that thing before I got shot down. That was kind of a personal triumph.

There was an announcement made as soon as we arrived at the Plantation by a general or high ranking officer from the North Vietnamese Army. They proclaimed there had been a peace accord signed between Kissinger and Lee Duc Tho. There would be a cease fire and prisoner exchange, and an agreement with North Vietnam to not continue their aggression against South Vietnam. Of course they didn't honor this. But, they did get a USA agreement to withdraw all of our forces from Vietnam.

There was an effort to make propaganda with this news as it was presented to the POWs. Cameras were positioned in the second story windows of the big house overlooking the courtyard. Upon assembling all of the prisoners in the courtyard standing in rank and file they had hoped to film the wild celebration when the news was read of the release. We anticipated their scheme.

So, our Senior Ranking Officer said, "Don't blink an eye. You stay in rank and don't talk. If there is any talking, I'll do it."

We all stood there. The pompous little general, who thought he was going to get his picture on national Vietnamese television reading this proclamation, came out well dressed in his snazzy uniform. He had a little lady interpreter with him. He opened the proclamation with great flair and read the proclamation informing us there would be a release completed within sixty days. We all stood there. We didn't move.

He asked his translator, "Did they understand that?"

The lady interpreter said, "Yes sir, they did."

He said, "I'll read it again."

He read it again and repeated the whole thing, receiving the same reaction from us. He asked the interpreter, "They did understand that, didn't they?"

"Yes sir."

He slammed his book closed and the two of them marched off without another word.

Our Senior Ranking Officer, standing in front of our formation, turned and said, "As you were."

We broke ranks and went back to our room as if it had been another dull day. We held our celebration until we were out of the range of the cameras. When we got back in our cells we gave each other hugs and confirmed our tour was coming to a close. We were jubilant but we certainly didn't want to show that in front of the North Vietnamese.

We spent two months there at the Plantation. It was good treatment there. We had regular food. It was only two bowls of soup per day but once and a while they'd try to give us a piece of sweetbread for breakfast.

They placed us in four-man rooms. They had the long rooms where you could get more than four per room, but for some reason they just kept it to four per room. They brought out some English novels, which was a new thing. We had never had anything to read the entire time we were there. And, in the final two months they provided a few paperbacks. The Godfather was one of them, I remember. That was very popular. We read it out loud in the room so four people could hear it. Then we would pass it to the next room. That way we all read The Godfather.

The North Vietnamese measured us for our *go home* clothes—shoes, pants, shirts, belt, a little windbreaker, and a small sports handbag, which they inspected very closely when we left because they didn't want us to steal anything and take it home with us from North Vietnam.

During that sixty-day period an official, who was circulating through the camp, came around to me with a cigar box full of wedding bands.

He asked, "Is one of these yours? You can take it home with you."

I said, "No." I didn't fly with my wedding band on.

"However," I said, "I would like to have my watch back."

He asked, "What kind of watch did you have?"

"It was a Seiko."

"I put one Seiko here and one Seiko here. How do you know which Seiko is yours?" he questioned.

I said, "That's easy. On the back of mine is an engraving."

"Engraving means....?"

"It means," I explained, "there is writing."

"What's it say?" he asked.

I said, "It says, 'Made in Japan'"

He nodded, walked off, and I never saw him again. But I doubt he made much of a search for my Seiko. By that time we all were in a pretty good mood. He was trying to return wedding bands; and some guys got their wedding bands back. We had no idea they were keeping them somewhere in a big cigar box.

Chapter 7
POLITICAL PAWNS

We were warriors stricken from the battlefield yet alive. We were huddled together and sustained with little concern from our captors. To the North Vietnamese communist we were a burden, nevertheless we were a useful burden in the fight for public opinion; we were a useful leverage to be applied against their opponent. Even greater than the lifeblood of the Ho Chi Minh trail was the force of the free world's public opinion—a world not under the subjugation of their Communist government.

In their world people who dissented simply disappeared never to be heard from again. In the free world people who dissented attracted the attention of a representative government. The winners of the battle of public opinion did so with a weapon much greater than all the bombs dropped on Hanoi.

The POWs held by the North Vietnamese were unwilling political chess pieces manipulated by their captors. Each opportunity to portray America as an unjust aggressor against the innocent peasants of North Vietnam was relished by their propaganda machine. Unfortunately, American representatives, many who were celebrities who hadn't a clue as to their part in the farce, were all too willing to advance their own personal agendas and became tools of the North Vietnamese communist regime.

With sentiment in the United States running strongly against the war, the anti-war crowd was bolstered and emboldened by a free media who did not hide the scars and flaws of their society but displayed differences, accusations, and even our mistakes in the bright light of day where everyone could see them. Only in a free society with a free press could the propaganda assault of the North Vietnamese Communists succeed so well.

A Bow From a POW

The North Vietnamese wanted to show the obedience which they had instilled (beaten) into an American prisoners by getting Commander Dick Stratton in his long pajamas and exposing him to some convention they were having. The cameras were rolling and Dick was instructed, "You must bow."

So, Dick went out and made exaggerated 90-degree bow to the four points to the compass: north, east, south, and west. And every American, who saw Dick doing that exaggerated bow on the six o'clock news, realized he was sending a message that this was done under duress and is total B.S.

Dick said, "Under the circumstances that was the best thing I thought I could do."

Captain Carrigan and the Women's Strike For Peace

POWs do not want visitors: regardless if they are reporters, peaceniks, clergy, or well-wishers. Without fail the visitors ask the wrong questions before the enemy: such as, How are you being treated? Do you get good food? How do you feel about the bombing of North Vietnam now? These questions place the prisoner in grave danger of extreme torture or even death if the truth is revealed. And yet, a patriotic American prisoner cannot compliment the enemy falsely. The dilemma cannot be resolved without painful consequences.

Captain Larry Carrigan, during my absence from the cell, had a devastating encounter with the dilemma. A visiting American group of ladies calling themselves, *Women's Strike for Peace*, entered the camp one night and requested to talk with a prisoner. Larry was hustled before them despite his protest. The women berated him for bombing hospitals and temples of worship. They insisted that they had seen it with their own eyes.

Larry was incensed and angrily responded, "You have seen no such thing. You have been given the *cook's tour* that all visitors get here in Hanoi. You've seen a pile of rubble with a fresh painted red cross on it." He then forcefully continued, "We never bomb civilian targets! My Wing Commander, Robin Olds, would have court-martialed me if I had bombed a civilian target. We had photos of the place to be bombed before striking it and photos taken afterwards. We would have been in serious trouble if a single stray bomb landed among the grass huts."

The women were stunned into silence when confronted with the truth in such a forceful manner. The stunned but enlightened women were quickly escorted away. Larry, however, was roughly returned to his cell with an admonition.

"Now you shall know pain!"

The following day he was taken to the Blue Room for torture. They tied ropes around both wrists; ran the ropes through eyebolts high on the wall and hoisted Larry off the floor, allowing him to hang there, suspended, for over four hours. Both shoulders were pulled out of the sockets. It was more than a month before he could raise his hands above chin level.

The Peaceniks

Most folks knew them as war protestors. We called them Peaceniks. We knew there were people protesting the war back home. The North Vietnamese extolled those activities that showed dissent with the Johnson Administration for their conduct in the war. If there was a march on Washington D.C. by the protestors, the North Vietnamese would somehow got a copy of a news magazine and reported that back.

I was once in an interrogation where the interrogator showed me a Time magazine. Up on a horse statue in some square, waving a North Vietnamese flag, was an American protestor…an antiwar Peacenik.

The interrogator said, "See, the protest. The American people are on our side."

I said, "No. That's just the way we do. In our country we are allowed to criticize our government….to dissent and make it known. Tell me what would happen if you went to Ba Dinh Square, climbed up on Ho Chi Minh's statue, and waved the American flag?"

He said, "No need to ask."

I replied, "No. You'd get shot. But, for us, that is just the way we do business in our country."

We got a giggle about one of the protestors we saw. They had humorous signs they were carrying. They were an amusement. We didn't consider them to be traitors. They were just Americans expressing their discontent with the way the war was being conducted.

Visit From the Peaceniks

I only had one occasion to be exposed to the peaceniks. In my initial months as a prisoner I spent some time in the hospital, where I received medical treatment to my broken femur. The odd thing about that was I stayed there a full thirty days, which was unusual because there was no need for that. They were holding me in abeyance until some progressive American came and visited Hanoi. Then they secretly shuttled me from Bac Mai Hospital into the Plantation, where Larry Carrigan was being held at this time in the room we called Showroom One.

The Bug met me and introduced me to the commander of prison camps in Hanoi, known to the prisoners as *the Rat* or *the Cat*. The Rat had a stern, serious look on his face as he circled me, growling out punchy statements in Vietnamese. The Bug translated that I had been brought back to the prison at this time to see some *"progressive American visitors"* who wanted to talk to a prisoner that had received the *humane and lenient treatment.*

"You must not say anything bad about your treatment here or the Vietnamese people. If you do," warned The Rat, "you will die here."

I was then thrust through a veil into a room where the cameras were running. To my surprise I stood face-to-face with Thomas Hayden, Rev. Jock Brown, Rennie Davis, Bob Allen, Carol McEldowney, and two others. The first thing I did was to attempt to avoid talking to them and being asked embarrassing questions like, "Are you being treated well? We see you've had medical attention. Is the food good?...etc." These are all things you can't really answer.

The first thing out of my mouth was, "Who are all you people and why are you here?"

That was exactly what they wanted to talk about with me. They went around the room and each of those guys made a five minute talk until we got to Tom Hayden and he made a twenty minute talk. He said things like he was not a pacifist but he wanted to stop the war and get everyone back home, including the Vietnamese captives.

I expressed my appreciation for their thoughts about my concern but told them my toes were beginning to swell up and I thought I had better go back to the room. They excused me from further interrogation as far as my treatment and any embarrassing thing that I might have to say. The clergyman did run up and ask me my wife's name and telephone number. And, she was pleased to hear that I had been treated for my injuries and seemed accommodated to the role of captive.

However, that did not prevent the propaganda specialist from snapping a photograph of a smiling Major Baker shaking hands with the anti-war representatives of the Peace Movement in the States.

I was never pressured to see any of the other peace groups after I saw Thomas Hayden and the other six people. However, we were aware that Jane Fonda was in town on a visit.

Jane Fonda's Visit to Hanoi

The camp commander at Son Tay, when I was there was nicknamed Blackie. We had no idea what their Vietnamese names were. He was the camp commander when they opened it in 1968 and was brutal to the prisoners until Ho Chi Minh died. But when I was there, during his second year of duty, we were back to a *live and let live* policy.

He came around one day and had an audience with me, Larry Carrigan, and Irby David Terrell; we were all in one room.

Through his interpreter he said, "Jane Fonda comes to entertain you. I will allow you to go see her."

We said, "No thanks."

He demanded the interpreter to repeat, "Jane Fonda comes to entertain you and I will allow you to go see her."

On behalf of myself and my roommates I said, "No, she doesn't come to entertain us. She comes to make propaganda. We don't participate in that. We won't go see her. We will take torture before we will go see her."

He looked at us with a steely eye and said, "You may do just that!"

He went on to another room looking for someone who would go see Jane Fonda. All of us refused. Word filtered back, "Nobody from Son Tay wants to see Jane Fonda." And, I think that is what happened all over the prisoner camp sites. Eventually a few people were duped into seeing her and she did have an audience or two but they were men we thought were too cooperative anyway.

167

Sonny Bono & the Bracelet

The Peaceniks didn't bother us. We did have an occasion once to learn about something else by reading Time magazine. Our captors were showing one prisoner a Time magazine article about a protest, or antiwar demonstration. A couple of pages over the prisoner saw a photograph of Sonny and Cher. He noticed Sonny had on a shiny simple bracelet. He took a piece of cellophane like a candy wrapper; he placed a tiny drop of water on that candy wrapper which made a magnifying glass of 25x power. This is something the POW knew. It enabled you to read tiny things.

He slipped that tiny cellophane around until he could read a name on that bracelet. It was a POWs name and recorded his shoot-down date. The bracelet was a new revelation to the POWs. Later he tapped the word out that there was obviously a movement aimed to popularize the names of the people who were being held captive. Sonny was wearing one of our bracelets! That simple revelation raised our morale a lot.

In my opinion, I believe the actions of the peaceniks and war protestors cost American lives. I think their actions extended the North Vietnamese resolve, who just might have folded up after the failure of the 1968 attacks on Hue. I have heard that from other analysts. We thought the *most glorious victories,* as they described them, over our squawk-box were really glorious defeats. They lost a lot of people. The 1968 Tet offensive might have been the end and it probably should have been.

The North Vietnamese had the peaceniks on their side making a lot of propaganda. However, not all of it was going in their favor. Something was happening to reveal to public the harsh treatment we had experienced in the early years. This truth about the torture made its way to the Paris Peace Talks. When it was revealed, their international reputation took a bad hit. So, I think the Peaceniks were a major factor which encouraged them stay in the fight.

Chapter 8
Homecoming

For nearly six years the North Vietnamese held us as *black criminals* and ignored the Geneva Conventions of 1954. Our cells were dark dungeons. We were rarely allowed outside of the cell. Our captors attempted to strip us of our identity by referring to us by an assigned one-syllable name. My appellation was not much more than a grunt and has no English equivalent. It was pronounced approximately as "cuh". I never found out if the name was given to me because it sounded like the last syllable of Baker or if it refers to their native word for "bridge". I was captured after destroying the Bac Giang Bridge for the second time.

Names and ranks were never recognized during our entire confinement, although our captors were well aware of who the Senior Ranking Officer was in each group. To further humiliate us, our captors insisted that we stand and bow from the waist to all Vietnamese: civilian, enlisted and officers alike. We rarely gave them much more than a head nod if we could get away with it.

We all had experienced unspeakable pain from torture, deprivation of sustenance and clothing, separation from friends and family, and humiliation to the point of unbearable emotional cruelty. And yet day after day we picked ourselves up, regrouped, and stood in formation as warriors, perhaps a little disheveled and unkempt, but united in spirit and purpose. And, then one day it was time to go home.

Getting on the Bus to Go Home

On the day we went home, they gave us our new clothes. They called out our name and we took our little satchels, which had nothing in them. In fact they checked them to be sure we didn't steal anything. Some guys managed to get home with their tin cup and I don't know how they hid that. I managed to bring home a souvenir from the camps by wearing my prison pajamas under my *go home* clothes.

We were put into mini-buses in certain order. It turned out they wanted us to be in our shoot-down order — not highest ranking order. It's obvious they were going to call our name out and we would be released in shoot-down order, earliest first.

On the trip out of the Plantation in the mini-van, there were crowds in the streets who were aware the POWs were being released. I think our captors had made some kind of news release of their own. The crowds threw rocks at us. They weren't big chunky rocks that did a lot of damage. But, the protest was there and it didn't bother us. We took flak coming in and we took flak going out. To the POW airmen that didn't matter.

They made one more propaganda attempt to capture us in a good mood on film. Before we reached the gates of Gia Lam Airport, which was the civilian airport where the Air Force was sending the C-141 transport airplanes to take us to Clark air base, they stopped at a little park and offered us cookies and beer.

They said, "You have a few more minutes before we should arrive and we will allow you to have cookies and beer."

We refused to accept that. There were too many cameras around there.

The ranking officer in our group said, "No, we are in a military formation. We don't take beer while in formation. We will stay on the bus."

We didn't even get off. We didn't relieve our bladder or anything. We said that this was formation and they just intended to make propaganda. They were looking for another way to show *the humane and lenient treatment*, which we had not received before. We certainly were not going to accept it now.

They took us to Gia Lam Airport where we dismounted from the bus and we formed up into two files in shoot-down order. When our name was called we marched forward and saluted to the American receiving officer, in this case it was Brigadier General Ogan.

I said, "Major Baker reporting for duty, sir."

He said, "By the way major, you're a lieutenant colonel now. Welcome back."

An escort officer came and took us by the elbow and said, "This way to the C-141."

And one by one we reported for duty. There was a large crowd there, including civilians, watching to see what our faces were going to be like, looking for anything unusual. We were strictly military in our decorum. Although, some of us could not help from grinning. We were determined to not make any propaganda for them at this final moment.

Among the crowd I saw the guy reading our name, who was The Rabbit. He was still a second lieutenant. He had been a second lieutenant six years earlier. I guess the promotional cycle is pretty slow there. The Rabbit was reading our names. I saw Soft Soap Fairy. He was sitting there among the Vietnamese dignitaries and translating from English into Vietnamese for them on anything that might have been said. I did not see any of the harsh interrogators though. The ones who caused so much torture were out of sight. They were not in evidence. Interestingly, I have since found in my research that these guards seemed to have disappeared.

Flight to Clark AFB, Philippine Islands

Three C-141 transport planes were sitting on the tarmac waiting for us when we arrived at Gia Lam Airport. The back ramps were down. If my memory serves me correctly, there were three planes. As we walked up the ramp and got on the C-141 there was the crew, a couple of flight nurses, a couple of airmen and the load masters. They handed us a cigar and welcomed us back.

We were very, very happy to see some friendly faces. We took a seat and didn't really celebrate until that plane got out on the runway, broke ground, lifted off, and the wheels left the soil of North Vietnam. That's when we tossed out hats, although we didn't have hats. In any case, we celebrated, hooped and hollered.

It took less than three hours for us to leave Hanoi and arrive on U.S. controlled land at Clark AFB, Philippine Islands. Those hours passed quickly. The crew had snacks for us and patiently answered our questions. We wanted to know who they were and what was going on in the states. They passed out magazines-- recent magazines.

Clark was another joyous occasion. They had us offload the airplanes in shoot-down order. Admiral Gaylord, CINCPAC, was there; he shook hands with each of us as we got off and welcomed us back. Then we walked over to an American bus. In doing so we walked by a lot of Americans who were assigned to Clark there and civilians.

As I was walking to the bus some lady hollered, "Kennett!" which is the name of my home town. She was from Kennett. She happened to be there with her husband who was an airman. She had her baby there with her. She wanted me to see the baby. So, I broke rank and walked over to the sidelines, gave her a hug, asked her name, and looked at the baby. She was there again when I came out three days later when I came to get on an airplane to be transported home. And, she had some souvenirs from the Philippine Islands for me. That was very thoughtful of her to do.

Whatever You Want to Eat

My group was the second large group out. The first group was old-timers and men who had been injured. They had processed through two weeks earlier. They informed the people at Clark that our stomachs were not delicate. We were hungry. We wanted steak and eggs and foods of substance. We didn't want pabulum. The medical minds were wondering how our digestive systems were going to be. We did not seek out ice cream sundaes or ice cream bars; we let that go by. We were really just starved for protein. All of us ate steaks and eggs and beans and hearty foods. So, they were geared up for our group when we arrived.

The mess sergeant there, it was a Navy base I think on this occasion, said, "Look, Colonel you can have anything that you want to eat. It's your first meal here; what's it gonna be? You can have anything except elephant ear on a bun, because we are out of those big buns."

I said, "How about two over easy and a steak--breakfast steak, a stack of wheat toast and a glass of milk?"

"Coming up!"

He was used to it. He got that sort of order all the time-- ham, steak, or sausage, whatever guys were hungry for. We sat there and talked. When I finished the second cup of coffee I said, "I think I'll just do it again." So he served me a second breakfast and that was my first sitting: four eggs, two steaks, wheat toast, jelly and bread and milk. We were starving. I was at that time a full fifty pounds lighter than I was when I was shot down. I was 165 lbs. when I went in during my fighting days and I came out at about 115 lbs.

We were at Clark AFB only three days. They had tuned up their teams. They looked us over for our health to see if there was anything critical they needed to look at right away. They had dentist and orthodontist on hand to build new teeth or a bridge if you lost your bridge or had your teeth knocked out while you were in prison. They did not want us to go home looking so beat up. If you were hollow-eyed or hungry they couldn't anything about that.

They had tailors available and made two uniforms for us — two class-A uniforms. An officer assigned to me had gone over my records; he went to the PX and acquired the appropriate ribbons to put on my new uniforms. I think it was a magnificent effort in those three days. We got measured up, and the tailors hit it hard. We suspect they hired every tailor in Angeles City, to show up there at Clark. They whipped out all those uniforms and put us back on the airplanes three days later in order to start winging us back to the nearest military hospital to our home.

Although there was tight security around the hospital to prevent well-wisher overload, Maree Jumper, wife of Major General Jimmy Jumper who was the 7th Air Force commander, came to welcome Bob Sawhill and me home. We had served in the 48th FIS at Langley AFB during Jumper's tenure as squadron CO of the F-106 outfit. That was back in the early 60s when General John Jumper, a past Chief of Staff of the Air Force, was a teenager called *Scoop* getting into mischief like climbing the base water tower to ride the rotating beacon around and around.

Maree explained that Jimmy was stateside getting treatment for lung cancer but wanted to be there. Maree asked if we were craving anything particular to eat. I responded PECAN PIE! There had been times in the prison that I thought I might never get another pecan pie. Maree recently had received a package of pecans from Paris, Texas, their original home. Sawhill wanted a chocolate cake. That night she baked the pie and cake and returned to the hospital the following day. Sawhill and I promptly ate the cake and took the pie to share with our other returnees. We will forever be grateful to Maree for her thoughtfulness on that occasion. I have not tasted a better pecan pie since that day.

175

Coming Stateside

As I winged my way back to the continental US I took stock of where I had been and where I was likely to go from this point forth. Most of the returnees wanted mostly to rejoin their respective services and attempt to pick up the pieces of our lives and careers. We did not expect ticker tape parades or special treatment.

Our return was not the "Johnny Comes Marching Home" that followed WWII. The mood of the country was one of great relief from an agonizingly long struggle within our own people as well as the Vietnamese. We wanted to return to our flying careers and continue to do what we do best---fly and fight.

But the flying and fighting was over and many; numerous changes had taken place during our long years of confinement. More than half of us had to face the emotional trauma of divorce. Some wives could not face the uncertainty of whether their husband would return or not. They pursued their lives independently with plans of granting a divorce if and when the POW returned. Fifty percent of the returning prisoners came home to a broken marriage.

Tragically, years were missed in watching our children grow. My two children were eight and ten years old when I left the country. They were fourteen and sixteen when I returned. The adjustment was agonizing. I had very little tolerance for boys wearing long hair and the teenage loud music and sloppy attire. Slowly we accustomed ourselves to the new life and moved forward.

Kelly AFB, San Antonio, Texas

I touched down at Kelly AFB in San Antonio, Texas. There were a half dozen POWs transferred to that particular base. My family had gathered there. From Clark they had advised my wife that I was in good shape and would return at such and such date and time to Kelly. So, she sort of gathered up my clan--my brothers or anyone else who wanted to come along. So, I had a little group of people waiting for me there.

We were each given a chance to talk on the microphone to a small gathered crowd, since there were only a half dozen of us and the press wanted to hear from us. This was something most of us had never done all the time we were prisoners of the North Vietnamese. We stepped up to the microphone and said, "Thanks for the welcome to San Antonio. We were all happy to be back."

We were required to report for duty in the hospital and be debriefed for the next two weeks. I was given space in the VIP quarters. Within a block or so I could walk to work. They some work to do on us. They had to get rid of internal parasites and had some internal treatments. They wanted to make sure our heart rate was going to come down. We were all so high when we got off that airplane we ran hyper for about a week. Then they noticed us all just settling back in. If there were diseases to treat they did that.

They had psychiatrists on the team who wanted to get a good long detail about your mental state. A cardiologist, who happened to be a bachelor, led my team. He discovered I had been informed by my wife that we were not going to live together or stay together. She had found another guy and he was waiting in the wings. All the POWs kind of anticipated that. It wasn't as big a shock to me as she thought it was going to be.

I said, "Okay, if that's the way you want to do it. You're going to miss some good years because I'm going to be a full colonel in four weeks. I'm already on the list."

It didn't matter to her; she had her life squared away.

The returnees rarely left the base. We were kind of under this team's observation, particularly our mental state. They were really worried about that. We took long survey tests. I remember one of those tests, having to do with my mental state, had 800 questions to it. The Air Force doctors were probing around trying to see if there was anything smoldering in there that they needed to treat me for.

What they discovered overall was the POWs had been in prison long enough to accommodate to our short-fallings. Anybody who yielded something in initial interrogation of captivity had terrific guilt feelings for about a year until he bumped into all the other guys who had the same kind of thing. Then he usually sorted through it and said, "Well that's what they told us would happen."

We did what they trained us to do. Nevertheless, it hurts inside to have to yield any damn thing to the enemy. If you wrote something that says you were sorry if you did something that killed Vietnamese, you're not the only one to ever say that. But, at the time it was part of our technique to keep from saying anything worse. We had accommodated to that; and now, we were gregarious. We talked about our activities in the camp.

Operation Homecoming and The Champagne Ride

After the two weeks of medical observation was completed, we experienced a program called Operation Homecoming. I went over to Randolph AFB, which is also in San Antonio, It's a training base which had a number of T-38 trainers at the 560Tactical Training Squadron. The staff at Randolph were authorized to give us a *Champagne* ride.

At Takhli, RTAB, when a pilot completed his hundredth mission, they brought out the fire trucks, hosed him down, gave him a bottle of Champagne, and took his picture. Everyone then went to the bar and had a great celebration. Well, we POWs never made it to that hundredth mission, obviously. We all got shot down on a shorter number of missions. Mine was the 61st mission.

But, the Air Force wanted us to have a similar celebration. So, they decided to take the POW up to fly in the T-38 in order to re-establish his identity as a pilot, which was cathartic. We really wanted that. Excitedly, I took the bird up for one hour. I did everything a T-38 could do--upside down, sideways, vertical, loops--I had a great time. When I came back down and stepped to the tarmac, I was wringing wet.

The IP in the backseat could tell I was a pilot—a seasoned one as a matter of fact. I had over 3,000 hours of fighting time. He just talked me through a landing and we taxied back in and put it in the chocks. He didn't even have to touch the controls after he started the engine. He was along for the ride. He said, "I'll start this thing for you Colonel and then you drive it."

We had a great time--that was our fun. A year later we found that OPEC had put the nation in great stress about using a lot of fuel. Most of the flying then on active duty was done by those who were going to be flying in the next war--captains and below. The rest of us received flight pay but no longer had to go down and get four hours of flight time monthly. The DOD waved that requirement, which meant returning airmen were probably not going to get to do much flying, unless the duty they drew required it. I took a job in the staff for my final duty assignment for four years. I didn't get to fly. But I realized flying was being done by the people that needed to do it. I am thankful the Air Force allowed us that last *Champagne* flight with the 560th. I'll never forget it.

Home to Kennett, Mo.

The people of my hometown, Kennett, Missouri, were wonderfully supportive in my turbulent days of readjustment to life in the US. They were consistent in their patriotism and unchanged in their pride of their boys in uniform. They invited me back home for a welcoming celebration that renewed friendships and bolstered my courage to face the new challenges of the new world.

The Mayor of Kennett presented me with the Key to Kennett as my high school friends gathered around to slap me on the back and welcome me home. I never felt prouder in my life. The memories of the hatred and violence imposed on me in North Vietnam began to fade. The healing began.

By the first week in May 1973 I was being invited to numerous meetings and honored as a returned POW. Texas Governor Dolph Briscoe contacted the returnees in Texas inviting us to Austin to receive a Joint Resolution from the Legislature commending us for service to our state and country. The VFW sponsored a lunch for us in order that we might have a chance to meet a few of the MIA wives that also were to be honored that day. I was pleased to be able to chat with these brave women who did not have a husband returned to them after the war.

That day changed my life. I met several MIA wives but the one that impressed me the most was Marjorie "Honey" Monteith Connolly, widow of Lieutenant Colonel Vincent Connolly who was killed in action (KIA) November 1966. She had waited seven and one half years to find out if he was among the returnees. I made sure I sat near her at lunch. She was in the company of Kay Uyeyama whose husband, Terry was a returnee and my friend from the prison.

From the luncheon site limos took us to the Capital. I rode in the limo with Honey, Kay and Terry. I wanted to know more about Honey and her family. To my surprise, she knew where Kennett, my home town in Missouri was. Her great aunt was from there as well and currently lived in San Antonio. We exchanged phone numbers so she could tell Aunt Josephine about me. She was sure Aunt Jo would want to meet the Kennett returnee.

I learned Honey had two children who were too young to have memories of her late husband. I learned also she lived in Austin near her brother, Dwight, and had just finished building a duplex there. I marveled at her courage and self-confidence. I discovered she was the daughter of Major General Dwight O. Monteith, USAF (Ret). She had a lifetime of military experience.

Her allegiance and devotion to her husband was not to be compromised until his fate was finalized.

Within a week, Aunt Jo called me and wanted me and my wife to come to San Antonio for dinner at La Louisian. When I reported that we were in the process of divorcing, she asked if she could have Honey join the dinner group. I was thrilled to accept the invitation to see Honey again.

The dinner at La Louisian was excellent and illuminating. I knew Aunt Jo's relatives personally and she knew mine. We were homies. Honey recalled that at the age of six she spent some time with Aunt Jo in Kennett. While there Aunt Jo took her to the municipal swimming pool where I was one of the life guards that summer. It was an established procedure to have everybody out of the pool for ten minutes. During that rest break, the life guards put on a display of comic dives. Honey had actually met me years ago. She was winning my heart every minute I was with her.

With Aunt Jo's stamp of approval of me, Honey accepted dinner engagements from me and our life forever changed as we bonded through our common interest and heritage.

Happily, our children meshed well. Honey's kids, Margie (8 yrs.) and John (10 yrs.) thought my teenagers, Mike (14 yrs.) and Melisa (16 yrs.) were cool. And, my teenagers had always wanted little brothers and sisters. The summer was full of parties and trips to the cabin at Lake Medina near San Antonio to swim and water ski.

I took a one-year assignment at Randolph AFB, San Antonio TX. We were becoming a close family of six. Before being reassigned to a Fort McNair, VA, for Senior Service Schooling, Honey accepted my proposal to marriage. The kids were for it. Although, Mike and Melisa were leaving behind some strong friendships. In the end, they made other close friends on the East Coast. I was appointed Director of Cost Analysis at System

181

Command Headquarters, Andrews AFB, MD, where I served for four years until we retired to return to Texas.

Melisa attended the University of Texas in Austin; Mike stayed in Maryland since he had married his High School sweetheart, Karen. Honey and I settled into a mini-ranch with Margie and John just west of Fort Worth in Parker County, Texas. We were blessed to have found each other at that time in our lives and merged families.

Honey's long wait in limbo was over. She was free to choose another man with whom to continue life. I was overjoyed to find a military-seasoned wife so well suited for my life. Margie and John needed a father and I needed them too. They were the age my children had been when I left for war. Happily, I got to see them go to dance lesson, play little league and all of the things I had missed with Mike and Melisa. I got to teach them the multiplication tables and fractions.

I became part of their life; became the Dad that they needed. Honey and I never let them forget who their father was and the sacrifice that he made for our country. Vince Connolly's photo and his display of medals hangs in our hall of honor to this day.

Actually, I retired because the military could not figure out what to do with the returning warriors. There was the post-war downsizing and organizational reconfiguring staff problems to be solved. And, the flyers once again practiced their craft of bombing and strafing on truck carcasses on the desert gunnery ranges, awaiting the call to battle another day.

The friendly State of Texas was a good choice for us to adapt to civilian life. Margie love riding horses and race around barrels with the high school rodeo team. John played tennis and made many friends in that group. Honey and I stayed busy building homes, golfing, flying, attending church and joining civic clubs etc. These are things military families often cannot do because of their duty requirements. For forty years we have created some marvelous memories of our life in Texas

However, I will forever have the memory of those brave men who flew wing tip to wing tip with me into battle, those men who died there, and those men who suffered with me the long years in the dungeons of North Vietnam will never be forgotten.

Over twenty-five hundred aviators were shot down during the war against North Vietnam. Five-hundred and one of the 601 POWs released were aviators; those were the ones of us who came back. The twenty percent survival rate was due to the lethality of the SAMs, MIGs, anti-aircraft fire, the primeval jungle, and the abject cruelty of our captors.

Paycheck for Five-and-a-Half Years of Captivity

There is no doubt that the Air Force was grateful for my service to my country. There is also no doubt that they have done admirably in taking care of my needs since my return and retirement. However, is it curious and amusing to consider the paycheck provided to the POWs for the time spent in captivity.

I was held captive for 2,031 days and upon my return I got paid for that time. This may be a well-kept secret of the Department of Defense, but, I was paid at the rate of five dollars per diem. They broke it down to two dollars for inadequate food, and three dollars for inadequate housing. McNamara and any other DOD member visiting Saigon in the war years were paid $89.00 per diem for their inconvenience of being away from their regular offices and families. The POWs worked for five bucks! We need to change that.

Did They All Come Home?

I have been asked if I thought we brought everybody home. Well, I do; and I'll tell you why. I had an opportunity to talk to the Soft-Soap Fairy on an occasion just before we left. He was one of the guys I mentioned that was so fluent in English. You couldn't get double entendre by him or anything like that. He was very bright. At that time he was a first lieutenant. He was thrilled about the fact that at last they had all the Americans off of Vietnamese soil.

In truth we had. They scratched around and found some who weren't even on Vietnamese soil. There was a Captain being held just across the border in China. He fell on the wrong side of the border. They managed to get him out of there. Everybody we had on our list as being alive and well and in Vietnam, which we had collected over all those years, came home — man for man.

Everybody loves conspiracy theories. They attempt to say men were spirited away to Russia or China. I don't think that is true. I mean, I saw it in their faces and heard it in their voices. "At last, the Americans are off our soil." This meant now they could do as they wished. Thus they overran Saigon in two more years. No, there is nobody left behind.

Going Back

I've also been asked if I would like to go back someday to visit, as if a trip to that place would have some sort of therapeutic benefit. The answer is, "No!" One of my friends went back. He had something he wanted to see.

One POW had been spared any bad treatment by the villagers, and he wanted to go find that village and say, "Thanks for treating me like a person." I thought that was very odd, because the villagers who got ahold of me did no such thing. They treated me like an animal. They did all the beating on me that they could possibly do. So, I didn't go back. I had nothing to say thanks for.

Senator John McCain has been back several times. But, not because he wants closure. He wants to smack them in the face with the treatment he had. His success in the life after Vietnam says, "Make propaganda out of this. Get your cameras out. I'm going to

talk. I'm going to tell your people about the way we were treated."
They don't like to see him coming.

Some of the guys were curious to go down and see what Son
Tay looks like. All they did was kick around in the rubble; I don't
think that is very interesting. It's not worth a trip to the Orient for
me to go see that--sorry, but no. I did like Bangkok. And, I
wouldn't mind going back and seeing some of the support people
in Thailand. But that will never happen. My life has become too
busy to do that. After all these years those people wouldn't still be
there. They closed the American side of the Royal base in Thailand
and there would just be nobody there.

It is a hollow place now. Those awful places, where my
friends and I struggled to stay alive and maintain a semblance of
self-respect, hold no magic for me. No, the magic is the memory
of brave and honorable men committed to a principle of
freedom that was instilled in us early in our lives in a myriad of
places scatted across this great land. The thing I return to as
often as I can, is the memory of warriors dealing with the hand
that was dealt them: who steeled themselves to **serve with
pride and return with honor.**

--End--

Appendix A
Photographs

Top left: Growing up in Kennett, Mo. In 1944. Member of the Boy Scouts and where the dream of flying began.

Top right: Shown here (left to right) are the Baker brothers: Dewey (15 yrs,) Mo (17 yrs,) and Lee (13 yrs) of Kennett, Mo 1949.

Center left: Bainbridge, Georgia, for Primary Flight School, April 1953. Standing in front of a T-6 trainer with (left to right) Jon Bowman, Bill McLaughlin (instructor,) and Mo Baker.

Center right: Lackland AFB, San Antonio, Texas, January 1953, Aviation Cadet Mo Baker

Bottom left: Takhli, Thailand, May 1967, Major Mo Baker's first combat mission into North Vietnam.

Top left and right: Major Elmo 'Mo' Baker, 357th Tactical Fighter Squadron, flying out of Takhli, Thailand, with a F-105 D Thunderchief 'Thud' fighter bomber. (1967)

Center right: Captain John Piowaty walks away from his damaged 'Thud.' "Any landing you can walk away from is a good landing."

Bottom: Group photograph of 357th Tactical Fighter Squadron. Major Elmo 'Mo' Baker, fourth from left bottom row. (1967)

Top left: Anti-aircraft gun and gunner. A Similar weapon shot Major 'Mo" Baker down on August 23rd 1967.

Top center: North Vietnamese propaganda photo of captured American Flyer. Most captured flyers were immediately stripped of all clothing.

Bottom left and right: Captured American flyers were often at the mercy of incensed villagers and mobs upon initial capture. Crowds often hurled physical blows as well as taunts and jeers.

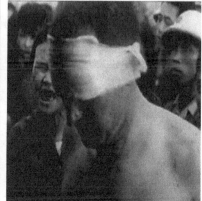

Top right: The entrance to the Hanoi Hilton from the street.

Top left: Aerial photograph of the grounds and compound of the complex known by the POWs as the Hanoi Hilton.

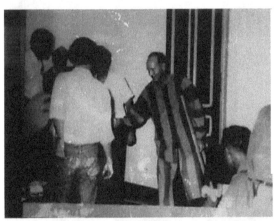

Center: Soon after release from the hospital from surgery on a broken femur, Major 'Mo' Baker was forced into a propaganda session with US Peace Advocates featuring Tom Hayden, Rev. Jock Brown, Rennie Davis, Bob Allen, Carol McEldowney, and two others (North Vietnamese propaganda photograph)

Bottom Left: Photograph showing Major 'Mo' Baker and Cpt. Larry Carrigan in a moment of domestic activity. Taken at the Plantation, where time was actually void of exposure to outside activities of recreational or therapeutic value... Scenes like this were usually for the North Vietnamese propaganda effort.

192

Top left: These two men were the most dangerous pair in the North Vietnam prison system. Apparently, they could do anything they wanted to the American prisoners, without high-office reprisal. The junior member on the left was called the Soft Soap Fairy. He was highly intelligent and was fluent in English. He was a lieutenant. The older man on the right was the Commander of Camps, Major Bai, known to us as The Rat or The Cat.

Illustrations: Lieutenant Commander John M. McGrath was a prisoner for six years. Rather than write an account of his captivity, he used his talent to draw illustrations of his experiences. (Prisoner of War – Six Years in Hanoi, Naval Institute Press)

Center left: The 'ropes' was a particularly favorite torture used, except if the prisoner had a broken limb. Then twisting and pulling on the broken limb would suffice.

Bottom left: Much of the time in the cell was spent watching for and monitoring the hallway for guards.

Bottom right: Communication through the Tap Code consisted of tapping knuckles on the wall with an ear to the tin cup pressed to the wall.

Top right: Jane Fonda's visit to Hanoi in 1972 earned her the nickname of "Hanoi Jane." Here she is shown observing an anti-aircraft gun used to shoot down American airmen.

Top left: Lt. Cdr Richard Stratton when forced to bow before the cameras, exaggerated the act and bowed dramatically in the four directions of the compass with the hope that it would signal home is actions were under duress.

Center left: Protests against the war increased in 1970 after National Guardsmen opened fire on war protestors on the campus of Kent State University in Ohio. Four students were fatally shot.

Center right: Although the POWs were aware if the protests at home, they were mostly ignorant of the volatile conditions which were escalating and the depth of distrust and animosity held toward American fighting forces.

Bottom left: Peace talks between the U.S, South Vietnam, and North Vietnam continued sporadically from 1968 until the accord was signed on January 27, 1973. The POWs and threats of bombings were used as bargaining chips and the actions of the war protestors encouraged North Vietnam to hold out for the most favorable position.

Top left and right: The POWs were released in groups. The order of release was longest held first. There were no smiles, emotional demonstrations or celebrations exhibited to prevent our captors from capitalizing on any opportunities to benefit from any release propaganda.

Bottom: As soon as the C-130 lifted from the runway of Gia Liam Airport, the POWs celebrated their return home.

195

Top right: A much thinner and lighter Major 'Mo' Baker shakes hands with Admiral Gaylord at Clark AFB, Philippine Islands. "Welcome home Colonel Baker," the admiral greeted.

Center right: Colonel Elmo 'Mo' Baker receiving commendations and certificates earned while serving as a prisoner of war. Presented at a ceremony at Randolph AFB, San Antonio, Texas in 1973.

Bottom left: Reunion of Thud drivers John Piowaty, 'Mo' Baker, and Jack Redman

At home and with his new family. *Pictured from left to right, back row*: Honey, Mo, Michael (14), Melissa (16), *Front row*: John (10), Margie (8)--1973

Retired Colonel Baker and his current wife Honey happily enjoying retirement in Texas

Appendix B
Joshua Fought the Battle
(A screenplay)

Joshua Fought the Battle
A screenplay written in solitude from the Hanoi Hilton
By Major Elmo 'Mo' Baker

Scene: A group of ragtag, dusty nomads standing on a sand dune peer across the Jordan River at a walled city.

Joshua: All right, get the navigator up here. Let's hear what he says.

Scurry, scurry, scurry. The navigator comes to the crest breathlessly.

Joshua: Okay, how about this place? Is THIS the promised land of Canaan?

Navigator: I don't know, Josh. Could be.

Joshua: DON'T call me Josh! Why don't you know? We have been wandering around out here in this desert for forty years. When are you gonna find it?

Navigator: Don't blame me Josh..er..I mean Your Grand Leadership. It would be easier if we had a compass.

Joshua: What's a compass?

Navigator: A thingy that tells which way you are going.

Joshua: Well why haven't we got one, for corn sakes?

Navigator: It hasn't been invented yet. Maybe you could put it a pitch to God for one the next time you two chat.

Joshua: Maybe. In the meantime we'll have to send some scouts down there to determine what that burg really is. First Sergeant, appoint two or three guys to check that town out after dark tonight.

First Sarge: Appoint? They will be fighting for the chance to see the bright lights. None of us has had R&R in forty years.

Joshua: Yeah, Yeah, I know. And all we have had for rations is Manna, Manna, and Manna. I've heard it all before, Sarge. For this job we need some real sneaky lads. How about sending Shadrach, Meshach and Abednego. Those scamps are always going AWOL.

First Sarge: They'll be perfect. But they may stay gone for a week.

Joshua: We'll camp on this side of the river and wait for their report. I'll try to call The Big Boss to let him know what we are up to.

****

Scene: *Joshua kneels inside his tent by candlelight intoning unintelligible prayers for an audience with God. Suddenly, an explosive puff of smoke fills the tent and God appears.*

****

Joshua: Cough, Cough, Cough, Hack, Hack. Wheeze. What is that smell? Brimstone? Why can't you use the door like everybody else does ?

God: I like the effect. I saw a magician do it once. He made an elephant disappear. I still haven't figured out how he did that. You called? What do you want now?

Joshua: We think we have found the Promised Land. I've got some guys checking it out now.

God: It's about time. Haven't you been out here in the desert for forty some years now? Gee whiskers, you are slow.

Joshua: Er....the navigator said he could work faster if you gave us a compass.

God: I haven't invented that yet.

Joshua: Couldn't you just crank one out for this occasion? We are sure getting tired of wandering.

God: That's not the way I work. Now, is that it? Anything else? I'm pretty busy running the universe these days.

Joshua: I guess not.

God: Keep in touch.

Poof. More smoke. More coughing and hacking.

****

Scene: *Three days later, near dusk, in camp when the three scouts return.*

****

Joshua: It's about time you scallywags returned. Let's hear your report.

Shadrach: Like you told us, Josh, we sneaked over there at night, scaled the wall and entered the city. We just happen to see a house nearby with a red light.

Joshua: How's that?

Shadrach: It was the house of a lady named Rahab. She was real friendly.

Joshua: I'll bet. Go on.

Shadrach: We hung out with Rahab for a couple of days whiled we checked things out. It is Canaan all right. The city is Jericho and it has a twenty-foot wall around it. It'll be tough to take that city.

Meshach: It'll be worth it, though, Josh. The women there have the biggest jugs……..

Joshua: Now watch that!

Meshach: …of milk and honey.

Abednego: He's not lying, Josh, they have HUGE…

Joshua: I said watch that talk!

Abednego: …bunches of grapes and stacks of baked bread.

Joshua: Okay, okay. You've made your point. Now get back to your folks. I'm gonna have to talk to the Big Kahuna on how to conquer the city.

****

Scene: Joshua goes into his tent and starts his prayer ritual that calls for another audience with God.

****

Poof, Cough, cough, cough, hack, hack, wheeze.

God: Now what?

Joshua: **Well it's Canaan for sure but a twenty-foot wall surrounds the city of Jericho. How we supposed to get through that? The thing is made of millions of fieldstones!**

Joshua: **Use the horn of the ram.**

Poof. Cough, cough, cough, hack, hack, wheeze.

Joshua: **There he goes again. Drops something cryptic on you and leaves in a cloud of smoke. Why does he do that? Busy with the universe. Busy with the universe**

****

Scene: Early morning gathering of the tribes of Israel.

First Sarge: Listen up to the Orders of the Day. (Aside) *They ain't gonna believe this.*   By orders of the Commander-in-chief, Josh..er...Joshua, we will march around the city of Jericho today seven times. Men first followed by the women.

Voice from the crowd: Alright! About Time, Sarge I got my new Keen Kutter sword all sharpened up.

First Sarge: NO SWORDS! Each person will carry a hymnal.

Crowd: What! You must be kidding!

First Sarge: (aside) *I told you they wouldn't believe it.* Joshua says we just sing for now. Now open your hymnals to page 185, <u>A Mighty Fortress Is Our God,</u> sing whatever part you like and MOVE'EM OUT.

****

Scene: Two Canaanite guards atop the wall around Jericho peer down on the spectacle.

****

First guard: Hee, hee, hee. Here they are today again. Seventh day in a row. Marching, singing, marching, singing. Strangest bunch of marauders I've ever seen. What do they plan on doing, bore us to death?

Second guard: Could be. I'm about bored to death now. But wait. Here's a new twist. They got rams' horns with them today. They are going to play us a little tune or something. Listen to that! Man, that's really awful. That's the worst vibes I've ever heard. It's even shaking these old field stones loose! We better get down off this thing! It's going to crumble!

****

Scene: *The walls have crumbled around Jericho and the Israelites have rushed in relentlessly blowing their horns.*

****

<u>Citizens of Jericho:</u> Alright, alright! We give up. You can have the city, just turn off that low-fi! Man! That's the worst music we have ever heard.

****

Scene: *Joshua kneeling in his tent has once again called for an audience with God.*

****

Poof. Hack, hack, cough, cough, wheeze!

<u>Joshua:</u> Dear God, we need to get you a new entry or get me a new set of lungs.

<u>God:</u> I get that all the time. What's up?

<u>Joshua:</u> Well, you were right. It worked. We captured the city of Jericho with the horn of the ram. First we put a little Psych war on them with hymn singing and marching for a week, then ta ta ta ta ta, the walls crumbled, we rushed in and they gave us the city.

<u>God:</u> Congratulations. I knew it would work. But what's all that ta ta ta ta stuff?

<u>Joshua:</u> Like you said, we blew the horn of the rams, the walls came tumbling down and we rushed in.

<u>God:</u> You dummy. I meant you get about forty rams, butt down the main gate, then you rush in with you Keen Kutters and do battle. Ta ta ta Ta! Geez! You could have been killed.

The end

(with apologies for the biblical inaccuracies. After all I didn't have The Book with me at the time)

Appendix C
Index